STORIES OF

Cats

AND THE

LIVES THEY TOUCH

Stories of Cats

AND THE
LIVES THEY TOUCH

Edited by Peggy Schaefer

Ideals Publications
Nashville, Tennessee

ISBN 0-8249-4628-6

Published by Ideals Publications, a division of Guideposts
535 Metroplex Drive, Suite 250, Nashville, Tennessee 37211
www.idealsbooks.com

Printed and bound in the U.S.A. by RR Donnelley

Library of Congress CIP data on file

Publisher, Patricia A. Pingry
Associate Publisher, Peggy Schaefer
Series Designer, Marisa Calvin
Copy Editor, Katie Patton

Cover photo copyright © Index Stock Imagery, Inc./Henryk Kaiser

10 9 8 7 6 5 4 3 2

ACKNOWLEDGMENTS

CARAS, ROGER. "Siafu" from *The Cats of Thistle Hill: A Mostly Peaceable Kingdom* Copyright © 1994
by Roger A. Caras. Used by permission of Simon & Schuster Adult Publishing Group. DAMIAN,
JACQUELINE. "One Hungry Cat," "Sasha's Tail," and "A Contrary Nature" from *Sasha's Tail*
Copyright © 1995 by Jacqueline Damian. Used by permission of WW Norton & Co. EDWARDS,
BILL. "Bill's Christmas Miracle" from *The Blessing of the Animals.* Copyright © 1996 by Philip
Gonzalez and Leonore Fleischer. Reprinted by permission of HarperCollins Publishers Inc. GERBER,
MERRILL JOAN. An excerpt from *Old Mother, Little Cat.* Copyright © 1995 by Merrill Joan Gerber.
Published by Longstreet Press. HERRIOT, JAMES. "The Christmas Kitten" from *The Best of James
Herriott.* Copyright © 1982 by The Reader's Digest Assoc., Inc. and used by permission of St.
Martin's Press, LLC in the USA and by Harold Ober Associates, Inc. for other territories. HUXLEY,
SALLY. "Crossing the Border" from *The Cat Who Had Two Lives.* Copyright © 1994 by Sally Huxley.
Used by permission of Donald I. Fine, an imprint of Penguin Group (USA) Inc. JOHNSON, PAM. "A
Lesson in Love" from *Hiss and Tell: True Stories from the Files of a Cat Shrink.* Copyright © 1996 by
Pam Johnson. Used by permission of The Crossing Press, a division of Ten Speed Press, Berkeley,
CA. KENDALL, GRANT. "Gary" from *The Animals in My Life.* Copyright © 1996 by Grant Kendall.
Used by permission of Wiley Publishing, Inc. MARCHANT, HELENA. "The Cat Who Was Always
There" from *Cat Caught My Heart* edited by Michael and Teresa B. Capuzzo. Doubleday, 1998.
TABER, GLADYS. An excerpt from *Amber, A Very Personal Cat.* Copyright © 1970 by Gladys Taber
and renewed ©1999 by Constance Taber Colby. Used by permission of Brandt & Hochman Literary
Agents, Inc. TULL, MARIANNA K. "Checkered Past" from *Cat Caught My Heart,* Doubleday, 1998.
Used by permission of the author. The Preservation Foundation, Inc. J. Richard Loller, Publisher,
on behalf of the authors, for permission to reprint "Killer Cat" by Arnetta Baugh, "Alamo
Encounter" by Mike Crifasi, "Lovey" by Betty Newsom, and "End of an Era" by Ellen Vayo, from *A
Curiosity of Cats.*

All other essays are from *Angels On Earth,* or from *Guideposts* magazine. Copyright © by
Guideposts, Carmel, NY.

All possible care has been taken to fully acknowledge the ownership and use of the selections
in this book. If any mistakes or omissions have occurred, they will be corrected in subsequent
editions, provided notification is sent to the publisher.

Contents

The Right Cat

at the Right Time

The Christmas Kitten

James Herriot

My strongest memory of Christmas will always be bound up with a certain little cat.

I first saw her when I was called to see one of Mrs. Ainsworth's dogs, and I looked in some surprise at the furry, black creature sitting before the fire.

"I didn't know you had a cat," I said.

The lady smiled. "We haven't. This is Debbie."

"Debbie?"

"Yes, at least that's what we call her. She's a stray. Comes here two or three times a week and we give her some food. I don't know where she lives but I believe she spends a lot of her time around one of the farms along the road."

"Do you ever get the feeling she wants to stay with you?"

"No." Mrs. Ainsworth shook her head. "She's a timid little thing. Just creeps in, has some food, then flits away. There's something so appealing about her but she doesn't seem to want to let me or anybody into her life."

I looked again at the little cat. "But she isn't just having food today."

"That's right. It's a funny thing but every now and

again she slips through here into the lounge and sits by the fire for a few minutes. It's as though she was giving herself a treat."

"Yes . . . I see what you mean." There was no doubt there was something unusual in the attitude of the little animal. She was sitting bolt upright on the thick rug which lay before the fireplace in which the coals glowed and flamed. She made no effort to curl up or wash herself or do anything other than gaze quietly ahead. And there was something in the dusty black of her coat, the half-wild, scrawny look of her, that gave me a clue. This was a special event in her life, a rare and wonderful thing; she was lapping up a comfort undreamed of in her daily existence.

As I watched, she turned, crept soundlessly from the room, and was gone.

"That's always the way with Debbie," Mrs. Ainsworth laughed. "She never stays more than ten minutes or so, then she's off."

She was a plumpish, pleasant-faced woman in her forties and the kind of client veterinary surgeons dream of: well off, generous, and the owner of three cosseted basset hounds. And it only needed the habitually mournful expressions of one of the dogs to deepen a little, and I was round there posthaste. Today one of the bassets had raised its paw and scratched its ear a couple of times and that was enough to send its mistress scurrying to the phone in great alarm.

So my visits to the Ainsworth home were frequent but undemanding, and I had ample opportunity to look out for the little cat that had intrigued me. On one occasion I spotted her nibbling daintily from a saucer at the kitchen door. As I watched she turned and almost floated on light footsteps into the hall, then through the lounge door.

The three bassets were already in residence, draped snoring on the fireside rug, but they seemed to be used to Debbie because two of them sniffed her in a bored manner and the third merely cocked a sleepy eye at her before flopping back on the rich pile.

Debbie sat among them in her usual posture: upright, intent, gazing absorbedly into the glowing coals. This time I tried to make friends with her. I approached her carefully but she leaned away as I stretched out my hand. However, by patient wheedling and soft talk I managed to touch her and gently stroke her cheek with one finger. There was a moment when she responded by putting her head on one side and rubbing back against my hand but soon she was ready to leave. Once outside the house she darted quickly along the road, then through a gap in a hedge, and the last I saw was the little black figure flitting over the rain-swept grass of a field.

"I wonder where she goes," I murmured half to myself. Mrs. Ainsworth appeared at my elbow. "That's something we've never been able to find out."

It must have been nearly three months before I heard from Mrs. Ainsworth, and in fact I had begun to wonder at the bassets' long symptom-less run when she came on the phone.

It was Christmas morning, and she was apologetic. "Mr. Herriot, I'm so sorry to bother you today of all days. I should think you want a rest at Christmas like anybody else." But her natural politeness could not hide the distress in her voice.

"Please don't worry about that," I said. "Which one is it this time?"

"It's not one of the dogs. It's . . . Debbie."

"Debbie? She's at your house now?"

"Yes . . . but there's something wrong. Please come quickly."

Driving through the marketplace I thought again that Darrowby on Christmas Day was like Dickens come to life: the empty square with the snow thick on the cobbles and hanging from the eaves of the fretted lines of roofs, the shops closed, and the coloured lights of the Christmas trees winking at the windows of the clustering houses, warmly inviting against the cold white bulk of the fells behind.

Mrs. Ainsworth's home was lavishly decorated with tinsel and holly, rows of drinks stood on the sideboard, and the rich aroma of turkey and sage and onion stuffing wafted from the kitchen. But her eyes were full of pain as she led me through to the lounge.

Debbie was there all right, but this time everything was different. She wasn't sitting upright in her usual position; she was stretched quite motionless on her side, and huddled close to her lay a tiny black kitten.

I looked down in bewilderment. "What's happened here?"

"It's the strangest thing," Mrs. Ainsworth replied. "I haven't seen her for several weeks, then she came in about two hours ago—sort of staggered into the kitchen, and she was carrying the kitten in her mouth. She took it through to the lounge and laid it on the rug and at first I was amused. But I could see all was not well because she sat as she usually does, but for a long time—over an hour—then she lay down like this and she hasn't moved."

I knelt on the rug and passed my hand over Debbie's neck and ribs. She was thinner than ever, her fur dirty and mud-caked. She did not resist as I gently opened her mouth. The tongue and mucous membranes were abnormally pale and the lips ice cold against my fingers. When I pulled down her eyelid and saw the dead white conjunctiva, a knell sounded in my mind.

I palpated the abdomen with a grim certainty as to what I would find and there was no surprise, only a dull sadness as my fingers closed around a hard lobulated mass deep among the viscera. Massive lymphosarcoma. Terminal and hopeless. I put my stethoscope on her heart and listened to the increasingly faint, rapid beat, then I straightened up and sat on the rug looking sightlessly into the fireplace, feeling the warmth of the flames on my face.

Mrs. Ainsworth's voice seemed to come from afar. "Is she ill, Mr. Herriot?"

I hesitated. "Yes . . . yes, I'm afraid so. She has a malignant growth." I stood up. "There's absolutely nothing I can do. I'm sorry."

"Oh!" Her hand went to her mouth and she looked at me wide-eyed. When at last she spoke her voice trembled. "Well, you must put her to sleep immediately. It's the only thing to do. We can't let her suffer."

"Mrs. Ainsworth," I said. "There's no need. She's dying now—in a coma—far beyond suffering."

She turned quickly away from me and was very still as she fought with her emotions. Then she gave up the struggle and dropped on her knees beside Debbie.

"Oh, poor little thing!" she sobbed, and stroked the cat's head again and again as the tears fell unchecked on the matted fur. "What she must have come through. I feel I ought to have done more for her."

For a few moments I was silent, feeling her sorrow, so discordant among the bright seasonal colours of this festive room. Then I spoke gently.

"Nobody could have done more than you," I said. "Nobody could have been kinder."

"But I'd have kept her here—in comfort. It must have been terrible out there in the cold when she was so desperately ill—I daren't think about it. And having kittens, too—I . . . I wonder how many she did have?"

I shrugged. "I don't suppose we'll ever know. Maybe just this one. It happens sometimes. And she brought it to you, didn't she?"

"Yes . . . that's right . . . she did . . . she did." Mrs. Ainsworth reached out and lifted the bedraggled black morsel. She smoothed her finger along the muddy fur and the tiny mouth opened in a soundless meow. "Isn't it strange? She was dying, and she brought her kitten here. And on Christmas Day."

I bent and put my hand on Debbie's heart. There was no beat.

I looked up. "I'm afraid she's gone." I lifted the small body, almost feather light, wrapped it in the sheet that had been spread on the rug, and took it out to the car.

When I came back Mrs. Ainsworth was still stroking the kitten. The tears had dried on her cheeks and she was bright-eyed as she looked at me.

"I've never had a cat before," she said.

I smiled. "Well, it looks as though you've got one now."

And she certainly had. That kitten grew rapidly into a sleek, handsome cat with a boisterous nature, which earned him the name of Buster. In every way he was the opposite of his timid little mother. Not for him the privations of the secret outdoor life; he stalked the rich carpets of the Ainsworth home like a king, and the ornate collar he always wore added something more to his presence.

On my visits I watched his development with delight, but the occasion that stays in my mind was the following Christmas Day, a year from his arrival.

I was out on my rounds as usual. I can't remember when I haven't had to work on Christmas Day because the animals have never got round to recognising it as a holiday; but with the passage of the years the vague resentment I used to feel has been replaced by philosophical acceptance.

After all, as I tramped around the hillside barns in the frosty air, I was working up a better appetite for my turkey than all the millions lying in bed or slumped by the fire; and this was aided by the innumerable aperitifs I received from the hospitable farmers.

I was on my way home, bathed in a rosy glow. I heard the cry as I was passing Mrs. Ainsworth's house.

"Merry Christmas, Mr. Herriot!" She was letting a visitor out of the front door, and she waved at me gaily. "Come in and have a drink to warm you up."

I didn't need warming up but I pulled in at the kerb without hesitation. In the house there was all the festive cheer of last year and the same glorious whiff of sage and onion, which set my gastric juices surging. But there was not the sorrow; there was Buster.

He was darting up to each of the dogs in turn, ears pricked, eyes blazing with devilment, dabbing a paw at them then streaking away.

Mrs. Ainsworth laughed. "You know, he plagues the life out of them. Gives them no peace."

She was right. To the bassets, Buster's arrival was rather like the intrusion of an irreverent outsider into an exclusive London club. For a long time they had led a life of measured grace: regular sedate walks with their mistress, superb food in ample quantities, and long snoring sessions on the rugs and armchairs. Their days followed one upon another in unruffled calm. And then came Buster.

He was dancing up to the youngest dog again, sideways

this time, head on one side, goading him. When he started boxing with both paws it was too much even for the basset. He dropped his dignity and rolled over with the cat in a brief wrestling match.

"I want to show you something." Mrs. Ainsworth lifted a hard rubber ball from the sideboard and went out to the garden, followed by Buster. She threw the ball across the lawn and the cat bounded after it over the frosted grass, the muscles rippling under the black sheen of his coat. He seized the ball in his teeth, brought it back to his mistress, dropped it at her feet, and waited expectantly. She threw it and he brought it back again.

I gasped incredulously. A feline retriever!

The bassets looked on disdainfully. Nothing would ever have induced them to chase a ball, but Buster did it again and again as though he would never tire of it.

Mrs. Ainsworth turned to me. "Have you ever seen anything like that?"

"No," I replied. "I never have. He is a most remarkable cat."

She snatched Buster from his play and we went back into the house, where she held him close to her face, laughing as the big cat purred and arched himself ecstatically against her cheek.

Looking at him, a picture of health and contentment, my mind went back to his mother. Was it too much to think that that dying little creature with the last of her strength had carried her kitten to the only haven of comfort and warmth she had ever known, in the hope that it would be cared for there? Maybe it was.

But it seemed I wasn't the only one with such fancies. Mrs. Ainsworth turned to me and though she was smiling her eyes were wistful.

"Debbie would be pleased," she said.

I nodded. "Yes, she would. . . . It was just a year ago today she brought him, wasn't it?"

"That's right." She hugged Buster to her again. "The best Christmas present I ever had."

One Hungry Cat

Jacqueline Damian

Where Charcoal came from, I don't really know. He just kind of showed up one day perhaps a year after our move to the country, a specter made manifest by the intensity of Sasha's wish for him to be there.

He came home with Sasha, who trotted in the door that autumn day as if there were nothing at all unusual about showing up for dinner with a strange black cat in tow. Charcoal scuttled along behind him to the food dish but kept one eye trained on me, ready to turn tail and run if things should turn ugly. It's scary to go where you're unsure of what your reception will be, unless you're very, very friendly—or very, very hungry. As it turned out, Charcoal was both.

He ate and ate. He would clean out his own dish, and wait politely until the other cats were finished so he could nose around in theirs for any dabs of cat food they might have left. Once in a while he stuck his head in Sasha's dish while Sasha was still eating. Perhaps because it was he who had invited Charcoal in, Sasha was tolerant of this breach of manners, at most giving him the kind of look you might give an uncouth dinner guest who was using his fingers instead of a fork on the mashed potatoes.

Lions and the other big cats understand the feast-or-famine mentality. They gorge themselves happily when they've downed some prey and then endure a fast until the next successful hunt, and this was the style that Charcoal brought to the food dish in my house. It took a good long while before he fully believed that the daily miracle of the ever-replenished kibbles would not give way to an empty bowl tomorrow.

Given their intense reaction to Sasha's arrival, I didn't know what to expect when Mimsy and Jean Arthur found yet another strange cat in their home. To my surprise, they didn't seem to mind. And clearly, Sasha had led the pantherlike newcomer to our door; they already seemed best of pals. Considering this a tacit okay from all three of the incumbents, I started feeding Charcoal, and he's pretty much been a fixture around here ever since.

One reason he fit in so well was his personality, which was definitely not Type A. Polite, affectionate, and easygoing, Charcoal was what you might call a plain-vanilla, no-frills feline—Shakespeare's "harmless necessary cat." Handsome without being beautiful, neither overly bright nor overly stupid, he wasn't much bother to have around except for getting underfoot whenever anyone went into the kitchen. He was a couple of years old, probably more, at this point, so he must once have lived around people. For unless a cat is lovingly handled and well socialized as a kitten, he grows up wary and skittish, the independent cat of myth, like my grandparents' Elmer, the one we called "wild," or the barn cats at the farm stand down the road.

Charcoal made himself pleasantly unobtrusive. He accepted without question that as an outsider, he was low cat on the totem pole, and in his dealings with the other three cats, he was deferential to a fault. He would quickly jump off any chair that one or another of them wanted to sit in, for example, locating an alternative spot that he always seemed to find just as satisfactory as his original choice. He followed Sasha around with obvious devotion, and was always in the mood for whatever adventures the other cat might cook up. If Sasha went out, Charcoal did too. When Sasha came in, so did he. And he left Mimsy and Jeannie alone.

With me and any other humans who might be around, he was almost painfully ingratiating, gratefully accepting whatever attention came his way and cheerfully putting up with indignities the other cats would never tolerate, such as being decked out in ribbons and dolls' clothes and getting toted around by one friend's young daughter. It was this child who gave Charcoal his name.

By this time, the Berlin Wall separating upstairs cats and downstairs cats was crumbling, and finally I decreed that the door between their enclaves would be opened. Any concerns I had about taking this radical step quickly vanished, for time had worked in my favor—and Charcoal's presence helped. As it turned out, this good-natured cat affected the balance of power in auspicious ways.

First of all, with Charcoal around, Sasha now had a buddy of his own, which cured him of constantly supplicating Mimsy and Jean Arthur with his offers—inevitably refused—of rough-and-tumble friendship. This was a relief to us all. Then, too, the cat constellation was more symmetrical with Charcoal in attendance. Instead of aligning themselves two against one, the cats now divided down the middle in two dual partnerships: a pair of older females and a pair of younger males—"the girls" and "the boys," as I took to calling them.

I've just been reading the zoologist Cynthia Moss's book on East African wildlife, *Portraits in the Wild*, and her report makes me think that male-male and female-female alliances like the ones my own cats formed might be the natural preference of cats. I may have inadvertently stumbled onto something that suited my domestic brood the day I let Charcoal in the door. Moss says that among lions, cheetahs, and leopards alike, same-sex chums are commonly seen but male-female friends are not—except, of course, during mating. This tendency is particularly distinct among cheetahs, who in terms of sociability fall somewhere between lions gathering in prides and leopards living alone.

When cheetah cubs are old enough to live independently, Moss says, a young female will frequently opt to remain with her mother. The two form a family unit, living and hunting together. But males are excluded from the feminine alliance, so male cubs often set off in the company of a brother, or else join forces with another young male they meet along the way who finds himself in the same situation. The cheetah mother is more skillful a hunter than even a full-grown cub, and she shares food with her daughter as the young cat hones her own predatory skills. But by bonding in pairs and hunting in tandem, the young males boost their own chances of bagging game.

Of course, it's always hard to generalize about cats, much less draw any conclusions from the example of their wild brethren. The big cats themselves continually confound the scientists who study them by exhibiting such a wide range of behaviors in their social lives and every other aspect of existence; you're seldom on solid ground making simplistic statements about them. How much more difficult the whole thing becomes among domestic cats, selected and bred by humans over several thousand years for physical and personality traits that we might consider appealing.

In the realm of male-female relationships, for example, I can't help but recall that Romeo and Bean, the cats of my childhood, lived happily together for many, many years. Unlike a cheetah mother, Bean saw no need to kick her son out of the house; and unlike a cheetah cub, Romeo didn't befriend the other male cats in the vicinity—not even Pinky, his half brother from an earlier litter, who lived around the corner with the Millers.

And friends who have long kept Siamese cats tell me this breed prefers living as male-female couples, behaving like loving spouses even when both of them are neutered. Their cats, Duchess and Cocoa, are the very picture of devotion, keeping up a stream of conversation, as Siamese do, as they follow each other around the house, as if to constantly monitor each other's thoughts and opinions. The more timid

Duchess frets and fusses terribly whenever bold, blue-eyed Cocoa goes outdoors without her.

Although feline life in my newly integrated household proceeded more calmly now than it once had, there were still some rough patches to get through. The main area of wrangling centered on me. As the only human in permanent residence, I was the one that all four cats turned to for strokes, literal and otherwise. And try as I might to attend evenhandedly to everyone, I had only so much time and attention to go around.

The rivalry was strongest between Jeannie and Sasha, for by now, like many a spurned suitor before him, Sasha had come to dislike the object of his affection. Just as neurotics sabotage themselves by behaving in precisely the way that's guaranteed to bring about what they most dread, so Jean Arthur's continued antipathy had turned Sasha into exactly the enemy she feared he would be.

I could understand Sasha's dislike; Jeannie was annoying. She still hissed and spat whenever she met up with him, and her histrionics were so out of proportion to the stimulus that even my sympathy was starting to wear thin. Also, she was an attention hog, a cuddler who wanted to sit on my lap or be carried at my shoulder, like an infant being burped, every waking moment of the day. Since Mimsy had never been a lap cat, her companion's obsession never was an issue in all the years the three of us lived together. But Sasha seemed to take it as a personal affront.

Sometimes he tried to force Jean Arthur from my lap by charging at her, either so he himself could come up for a cuddle or—at least so it seemed to me—just for spite. At other times he would acknowledge the fact that Jeannie got there first, while making it plain he was far from pleased. His two favored ways of conveying this message were to march ostentatiously to the front door and demand to go outside (which served to evict Jean Arthur from my lap, momentarily anyway, while I got up to let him out) or to sit across the room from us, on top of the TV, and glower at the distasteful spectacle before him.

Charcoal remained on the sidelines as this battle of wills went on. He must have known that with three other cats vying for my attention, he didn't have much of a chance. Charcoal was the cat in the middle, the silent onlooker, and I didn't pay him too much mind. I fed him and let him in the house, but I told myself that despite evidence to the contrary he was not really "my" cat. Who needed four? Three cats were more than enough to handle, and sometimes too much. When anyone asked how many cats I had, I always said three and a half. Charcoal was the half.

Of course, this was partly his own doing. Charcoal didn't stick around full time, but would show up, hang out with Sasha for a few days or a week, and then disappear for a while. I see in retrospect that this pattern was just like roaming Romeo's; it signified nothing more than "unneutered male." At the time, though, I nourished the hope that Charcoal might have a real home elsewhere, and was only stopping by in a series of prolonged social calls.

But in the months following Charcoal's first appearance at my door, three events occurred to change the picture irrevocably. First of all, Mimsy and Jean Arthur both died, leaving the planet the summer they were both fifteen in pretty much the same order in which they had entered it. Mimsy went first. She suddenly grew quite thin, and before I had a chance to get her to the vet's, she left the house one morning and never returned. I scoured the neighborhood looking for her to no avail, and I assume she must have gone away to die.

Jeannie, meanwhile, had been a sickly little thing all her life, spending more time than any cat should at the vet's. She deteriorated fast after Mimsy's disappearance, and finally I felt I had no choice but to have her put to sleep, the first (and, I hope, the last) time I ever had to make that wrenching decision. Maybe it was my obvious distress, or maybe it's something they always do for bereaved owners; but the vet and his assistant kindly sent me a sympathy card after this awful event.

The next trauma was Charcoal's. Following a fall and winter during which he was at home with me and Sasha more often than he was away, Charcoal suddenly showed up one fine spring day with a broken back left leg. Animals have an amazing tolerance for pain, and Charcoal was stoic about his injury. He seemed just as cheerful—and just as hungry—as usual, despite the fact that he was hobbling around with his leg hanging weirdly off the ground at a crooked, unnatural angle. When I took him to the vet's, x-rays showed that shotgun pellets had shattered his thigh bone. I never found out who was responsible, or whether Charcoal was shot intentionally or by accident.

Dr. Dubensky wasn't sure if he could save the cat, but in the end he performed remarkably delicate surgery, and Charcoal is still with us to vouch for the vet's skill. He barely even limps. In fact, the only visible consequence of his injury is that the claws on both of Charcoal's back legs no longer retract, a trait he shares with cheetahs and with dogs.

I decided to have Charcoal neutered during his three-week stay at the veterinary hospital to curtail his wandering (and to ensure that he wouldn't add to the population of unwanted kittens) and thus, finally, assumed responsibility for this wayward animal. However it had happened, Charcoal was officially mine.

Alamo Encounter

Mike Crifasi

Cats know nothing of the human condition, nor would they care if they did, I think. They are free animals, quite content to roam wherever and whenever they choose, with not a thought as to anyone else's concerns on the matter. They tread upon whatever gains their fancy—their only aims their own amusement and, occasionally, survival. Perhaps that is why we humans look upon them with such awe and such longing.

As I sit here in San Antonio, it is those thoughts that are passing through my head. I'm in the Alamo—a somber reminder of human cruelty and destruction, even on American soil—sitting on a bench across from the memorial wall. This is where I was able to find a much needed rest from trudging along after my dad through the old mission. My dad is quite the history buff and appears so enwrapped in the experience, that he has not even noticed my absence from his flank. I am quite happy to be able to slip away, and I doubt if it would bother him at the moment if he knew.

It's not as if I don't understand or appreciate the depth and impact of this place, nor do I have anything but the deepest respect for those who gave their lives to defend it.

It's all just a little too heavy for me, leaving me feeling drab and depressed. I suppose I'm too emotional to look at it objectively and with interest. It just seems too sad and it brings me down.

So here I am, on a rather pleasant Sunday morn in San Antonio, looking at the mission walls and rich vegetation within this historic site, resting my weary legs and feeling, well, a little down.

Suddenly, I see it.

And I can hardly believe my eyes.

Making its way between the small ferns planted before the wall covered in maps and names, disappearing and reappearing behind the legs of tourists who pay it no attention, is a feline with smooth black fur and white patches. My heart lightens as I gaze in amazement at what seems to be such an out-of-place visitor. It stops and sits up, its tail swaying lazily from side to side behind it, right across from the little bench to which I have laid temporary claim.

I still cannot get over my shock that such a creature would be found on this hallowed ground. I am also quite unaware that this new presence has swept away my disillusionment, although I'm sure some small part of my soul is very thankful for that. I sit up a little, interested in what the cat will do next.

It just continues to sit and stare at me, tilting its head a little to the side, as if more amused by my attention than I am surprised by its entrance. Its eyes have that squinted look that, in people, means that the sun is bothering them and, in cats, that they are either coming from or going to a delightful nap.

So we have acknowledged each other's presence, but what now? Like too-shy teenagers in the thralls of young love, we continue to sit there. I am, in my own small way, a "cat person," so I do what any person of that guild would do, I dumbly attempt to call it over to me.

I also continue to stare right at it, hoping that it can somehow sense in my stare that I am a companion, a kindred spirit. While my gaze holds its focus, I lift my right hand just the smallest bit from its perch upon my thigh and begin to rub the first two fingers and thumb together gently, in what I guess must be a universal cat-call motion. I don't really expect much out of it, but it gives me something to do, something better than dwelling upon the history of my own kind sometimes best left forgotten.

That's when my new feline friend surprises me. After another look, head nod, and further squinting of its sea-green eyes, it begins to walk toward me.

A few nearby tourists take casual notice, although not my father, who is too deeply entrenched in who shot at whom, where, and how many times. Right now, all my attention and consequential excitement is placed upon this strange cat, that somehow, I am getting to come and spend time with me.

It reaches me and stops. It then looks up at me with a curious stare and sits. I stare back, and it seems like an eternity before I notice it doing the signature bunching-up move cats do before they are about to spring upon something. After a few good moments of preparation, it leaps onto the bench beside me.

The cat stands there for a moment, apparently still trying to decide if it really wants to trust me, holding its ears back and its body prone. Then, cautiously, it leans forward, raises a paw with white ends like a sock, and lays it upon my leg. The rest of its limbs are soon to follow, and suddenly I have an unknown cat in a strange city rubbing against me and requesting attention. And who am I to deny that?

Rubbing behind its ears, under its neck, and along its back, I continue to be amazed at this small miracle. Maybe I just like cats more than the next person, maybe I just crave companionship, but regardless, I tell you, this cat purring under my touch is bringing me more happiness than anything else I have come upon today.

People have turned to look. Passersby who have happened to witness the encounter comment softly about the cuteness of the situation. It's the same reaction the newborn brought into the relative's room for the first time receives. Now the whole congregation of people around the wall are watching our interaction, even my dad, who is finally looking father-like as he raises the camera for what is sure to be a refrigerator masterpiece when we get back home. I don't need to look up, and the contented feline pays no heed to anything but finding the best angle from which to receive maximum stroking, but I think we both feel the power of our simple act of trust.

A whole group of strangers—young couples, old gentlemen, and the occasional wide-eyed child—have turned from their sad contemplation of one of man's tragic events, to the greatness of an everyday event at hand. They have been taken from their isolation and have been brought together by seeing two strangers come together over nothing but pure goodwill and the wish for some simple enjoyment. And in those minutes, their cares are forgotten, and so are mine.

I pet the cat some more, and eventually the bliss passes. The onlookers move on; my father turns back to his wall and his names. After a final look, he begins to move on too, telling me that it's time we finished our tour.

A sadness washes over me as I finally admit to myself that I will have to leave this new friend. Still, it is totally unlike the cloudy haze that had gripped me before the cat strolled so casually into my life. It is a bittersweet twinge in my soul, a knowledge that while leaving it to continue its roaming and carefree life will hurt, I will always carry the memory that we spent this magical time together, and for a while our experience touched lives other than our own.

I stroke it one more time and then stop. It opens its eyes and looks up to me, and I swear it was saying yes, it understood everything I had thought and felt, and the impact had been the same for it. It's as if it understood and accepted it better than I, in that infinite wisdom any cat person can tell you felines have. The hope from that thankful gaze, I think, will stay with me always.

I set the cat down and after a final grazing of my legs, it moves on, tail raised and swaying gracefully. I rise and smile after it, thanking it in my mind and wishing it a good journey. I move on, feeling all the better that it has touched my life, however briefly. I believe for the moment that somehow, everything from now on will be okay.

Old Mother,
Little Cat

Merrill Joan Gerber

On this particular December morning, I am having enough trouble as it is: troubles of the heart that can't be fixed as well as troubles that can be. Even as I kick an old towel around on the kitchen floor to sop up the leak from the dishwasher, I'm thinking of what I need to take to my mother today at the nursing home: mints, a small pillow for her paralyzed arm, the sharp scissors so I can give her a haircut—if the nurses have been able to convince her to sit up in the wheelchair for a while. I'm also making mental lists of the errands I have to run afterward.

So the floor won't flood, I grab the dripping towel and run with it to the back door. I do this automatically—I wring it out and hang it over the pool wall, I gather up the dry one from yesterday to lay it down under the leak. J., my good husband and man of the house, definitely plans to fix this leak; but I don't think he has the faintest idea of what is wrong. Still, he says he's not ready for me to call a plumber. He wants to think about it a little more.

My mind is everywhere at once; I need to do food shopping at the market after I see my mother. My college girls are coming home for the Christmas break in a few days, and I'll need lots more grains tables. (J. and I haven't quite given up our meat and buttered potatoes diet, though we've improved.)

I stand outside near the pool for a moment, watching the water drip from the towel and looking around at the bleak winter view—at the dead leaves on the deck and the pecans from the tree floating like black beetles in the icy water.

A squadron of crows descends on the lawn, calling out with loud caws for others to join them to forage for newly fallen pecans. In this gray morning hour, the large birds, bent forward over their task, look like black stones on the paltry stretch of winter grass.

And it is then, just then, that I hear the cry. It seems to come almost from the tips of my toes—the saddest, most forlorn moan I have ever heard.

"What is it?" I cry automatically.

But there is only silence. Did I imagine it?

I look around now, alert and aware; I sense nothing but the faint movement of the trees in the chill winter wind (a cold wind, even for California) and the occasional clack of a crow.

I am about to go inside, when the sound comes again. It's an urgent sound, as close to a plea as it can be without words. Is it our old cat, Kitty, hurt or trapped? Even as I imagine this, Kitty appears on the pool wall, walking in his slow, majestic way, his great, old, gray coat thick and fluffed with winter fur. When the cry repeats itself, we both hear it. Kitty freezes and stares at my feet. Nothing is there but patterns on the darkened concrete— the splotchy water stains that are dripping from the towel.

"What is it, where are you?" I say again. The cry is vocal now, loud, full of pain, desperate. Then I see something just behind the wire screen that covers a square opening under the house, a crawl space to a place where no one ever goes. Something is pressed against the grids. I kneel down and see a pair of round, green eyes looking back at me. They are both like little mouths open in terror.

"Oh, no," I say to Kitty. "It's some kind of creature."

The creature opens its mouth to cry out as if to verify this, and I hear the sound clearly and recognize it for what it is. The meow of a kitten. *No. No, I won't think of it. Absolutely not. I won't consider it. I am done with these matters. I don't have the strength for it.* I've done my duty: three children, a dog, dozens of mice, fish, birds, and two cats, one of which (Korky, the Beloved) we buried two years ago in the backyard at a solemn funeral rite. Only old Kitty is left, and when he dies, which J. hopes will be in our lifetime, we can finally travel somewhere without endless arrangements and worries.

The hackles are up on Kitty's back; he wants no new friend, either. Fine. We're in agreement.

Go inside and forget about him. The next time you come out he'll be gone.

Even as I'm thinking this, I'm trying to pull the screen away from its frame, saying, "Shh, shh, don't be afraid, little one, you'll be fine, no one is going to hurt you." *Whose voice could this be? It can't be mine, not when I'm thinking something else entirely!* With a great heave of my arm, the rusted, old screen comes away and the green eyes withdraw and vanish. I get a glimpse of something hopping, bunny-like, away into the dark recesses under the house.

My heart is full. I feel passionate, a long-gone sensation I barely recognize. I'm energized, full of purpose. I rush into the house and get a bowl and fill it with milk. I shake some of Kitty's dry food into a plate. I don't say a word to J., who is reading the paper at the kitchen table. This will have to be a secret between me and Kitty, who has followed me into the house and whose eyes are narrowed as he watches me.

Outside again, I set the food dishes down in the place where I first saw the green eyes, in the hollow, dark place under the house, on plain dirt. In the twenty-five years we've lived here, I've never really looked into this hole, into the cavernous darkness there. How could a kitten have gotten underneath, into this inhospitable cave? And why did he stay?

I wait, watching the food bowls, but there is no sound, no motion. Even Kitty, seeing that I have set out food, and having a passion for almost nothing else, does not try to venture there.

I look at him, fat and furred, in his thick, gray coat. His enormous paws are like cartoon drawings. He, too, appeared in our lives as if by design on a day at least twelve years ago. J. was in the driveway with our daughters, all of them washing the station wagon. The kitten wandered shyly up to the bucket of suds and pitifully began to lap at the soapy water. J. shooed him away and a chorus of protests arose:

"Ooooh, the poor thing."

"Look how hungry he is!"

"Oh, see how he's shivering."

"Don't anyone feed him," J. warned, "or he'll never leave."

Exactly! Our three daughters, as if by signal, dropped their rags, ran into the house, and in half a minute brought out a feast: cream and raw eggs and bits of salami. The kitten ate ravenously, making gasping, almost sobbing sounds.

"He shouldn't eat so fast," said my youngest. "He might have to throw up." She then saw that the kitten had seven toes on one paw, and eight on the other "Oh no, he's a misfit," she cried. "We have to adopt him, so he'll feel loved."

"Don't even consider it," J. said. "And don't give him a name."

"We'll just call him Kitty," she told him, as if to reassure him that a generic title could prevent ownership. And so she did call him Kitty. And so did her sisters. And so did I. And so he has been called ever after.

Now I say to him, after all these many years that he has been called, merely, Kitty, "Don't worry, Big Kitty, we love you too." And I realize that by naming him thus, I've just made room for one more.

His Mysterious Ways

Mary Nichols

My daughter, Tori, knelt in the parking lot of our condo petting a scraggly, black-and-white cat without a collar. "Can we keep her, Mom, please? I already know what to call her. Oreo."

"Honey, you know I'd love to help this cat. But . . ."

We already had two cats. There was simply no room for this bedraggled little stray. But how could I tell that to my child?

"Where else is she going to go, Mom?"

"All right," I sighed. "We'll take her for the time being. But just remember, she can't stay. God will find a loving home for her somewhere."

Those words clearly made Tori feel better, but I couldn't help wondering if I'd just gotten myself into a fix. God had better things to do than worry about where to put this black-and-white orphan.

We called a local shelter with a description of the cat and put an ad in the lost-and-found section of the paper. I phoned all my friends, even though I knew what their answers would be. Nobody wanted a cat. Each time I heard Tori call the cat "Oreo," I cringed, knowing how attached she was getting.

In desperation, I e-mailed the other teachers at the school where I work. One responded immediately.

"My student's cat was hit by a car recently," she wrote, "and she really wants a new one. Could she come by and meet yours?"

Tori wasn't at all thrilled when I told her the good news.

"How will we know that's the right home for Oreo?" she asked.

The girl and her mother came to the house that night. Tori held the cat protectively in her arms as the other girl stroked her—clearly smitten.

"She's beautiful," the girl said. "I'd love to take her. I know just what I want to call her too: O.J."

"Why O.J.?" Tori asked doubtfully.

"'Cause my last cat was named Oreo. This one would be Oreo Junior."

My daughter looked from the girl to me with a speechless smile. Then she kissed Oreo goodbye and handed her over to her new owners.

Cats and the

People They Own

Sasha's Tail

Jaqueline Damian

The single thing that everyone who meets Sasha notices first is the way that he carries his tail. He typically walks around with this magnificently long, luxuriantly feathered appendage held proudly aloft like a flag, a posture that augments the sense of grandeur with which he presents himself.

This tail is indeed a remarkable organ. Functionally, it serves him as a kind of rudder. Repositioning itself as the animal jumps or falls, the clever tail is largely responsible for a cat's fabled ability to land on his feet. Aesthetically, it's a thing of beauty, two inches in diameter and wispy as milkweed. And expressively, it's an eloquent tool. Sasha speaks volumes with his tail. He flicks it in what can only be read as impatience when annoyed, and he whips it about wickedly when he's mad. When he concentrates on something, the tail concentrates too. It stretches out rigid behind him as he stalks prey and twitches thoughtfully as he stops, ears pricked, to listen for some elusive sound.

Outdoors, he raises it in a visual "Hello!" as soon as he enters a magic circle of his own imagining that extends, like a spotlight beamed on a lone performer, three to five feet around wherever I happen to be standing. "Here I am!" the tail says, in a throwback to the signal of recognition kittens give whenever they see their mothers—a mannerism that reminds me of the colorful flags that Sistine Chapel tour guides carry so their groups can easily spot them amid the swirl of other tourists. (The analogy is not so far-fetched: mother leopards with cubs trailing behind them in the tall grass of the African plains loop their tails up and forward over their backs; since the underside of a leopard's tail is almost pure white, it acts like the beam of a lightship guiding sailors through a grassy sea.)

There is a protocol to the raising and lowering of the tail. This is a conscious greeting, not a random one, for Sasha typically lifts his tail only if we have made eye contact or he is walking directly toward me. And only within a certain range. Outside the circle that Sasha envisions around me, he keeps his tail down; when he crosses the perimeter, it rises as surely as the tide. Like the moon, I affect its ebb and flow, for I have the power to expand the circumference of the circle with my voice. When Sasha hears me speak, especially if I say his name, he immediately lifts his tail in response, even if he's outside the usual confines of the circle. Not too far outside of it, though. If he is, say, fifty or a hundred feet up the path in front of my neighbors' houses, he bounds toward me with tail stretched parallel to the ground, and only raises it when he is ten or fifteen feet away.

When Sasha is investigating something—examining the

crevice in a stone wall that a chipmunk has just ducked into, for example—it will not let him be. I speak, and up the tail goes, but it's down again in an instant. I say another word and it rises again—and just as promptly falls. The tail has a mind of its own. It's like a very polite person who feels he must return your greeting even as you interrupt him in the middle of some important task.

But the tail has another tale to tell. It's also a marker of status and authority, and to fully understand Sasha's character, status must be taken into account. For Sasha is top cat. He is the boss cat in the household, the big enchilada, the cat-in-chief. He is the alpha cat, to borrow the term biologists use to denote a dominant individual in, say, a wolf pack, and as such he is daily preoccupied with questions of status and submission.

You don't have to be a particularly astute observer to notice this cat's air of authority. It hangs about him like an aura—charisma, feline-style. I myself fell into its thrall that dark October night when Sasha introduced himself outside a Rhode Island restaurant and convinced me, against all rational judgment, to take him home. Tigger saw it too. For the first couple of weeks after he came to live with us, the kitten would literally quake in his boots whenever he caught sight of Sasha, even though the top cat was not at all aggressive toward him. At dinnertime Tigger ducked into the narrow space between the pie safe and the kitchen workstation, and poked his head out just a little bit to sneak a peek at Sasha as he ate. Nothing could induce him to come get his own food until the top cat had licked his chops and gone back outside.

Sasha has star quality. You see it in his face, in his posture, in the self-confident way he moves through the world. Sasha doesn't walk, he struts. This is partly due to biomechanics—his back legs are slightly knock-kneed, giving him a swaggering, gunslinger's gait—but it's just as much a matter of attitude. You see it in his self-assured dealings with other cats, with humans—even with dogs. And you see it in his tail.

There's something so prideful—so bold—in the way Sasha carries his tail that it seems to shout self-satisfaction and high spirits. Tail erect, he's Jupiter brandishing his trident, a drum major leading a parade, or Charlie Chaplin twirling his cane. My friend Beth, newly returned from a wolf-watching trek in northern Minnesota, found a parallel in the upright-tail stance that tells observers (and other wolves) at a glance who is top animal in a wolf pack, and her interpretation gains credence in light of the fact that Sasha raises his tail not only when he greets me, but also when he approaches Charcoal and Tigger (who don't follow suit in approaching him or each other, although they do raise their tails for me). The kittenish explanation might do for a cat saying hello to a person, but it doesn't hold water for a top cat greeting an underling.

It's hard to read this tail when it comes to relations with the other two cats. Sometimes Sasha saunters up to them with tail held high in a friendly greeting; the next thing to happen will be head bumps, the feline equivalent of shaking hands. But sometimes he approaches with tail high and body language that seems to bristle, then jumps on top of them and wrestles them to the ground in a show of dominance. Let's hope Charcoal and Tigger are better at decoding the tail's meaning in regard to themselves than I am.

Gary

Grant Kendall

As a country vet, I know that horses can be dangerous. While I have never been killed by a horse, I have been injured, and I was once put out of commission by a panicked yearling. My old and true clients, Roger and Susan Glendon, have boarded horses on and off for years for Max Dammer—it was one of his horses that got me. Max wanted me to come by and do a Coggins blood test on his new yearlings before they were sent on to Aiken, South Carolina, to be broken. We were careful, and although some of the horses acted pretty nasty, the first nine were bled with no damage to either horses or people.

Number ten, though, was something else entirely. As soon as I stuck the needle through the colt's skin, he exploded. To this day, neither Roger nor I know exactly what happened, but somewhere in the melee I was kicked or struck on the outside of my right knee, forcing it to bend inward. This is not a normal knee function.

We didn't get the test done on the colt that day or for the next ninety days, because that's how long I was out of action. I was put in a brace and grounded while my knee healed.

At the time of my injury, Gary, our socially maladjusted female cat, had lived with us for many years; it must have been five years, anyhow. Many times we would go days without seeing her. She was about three months old when we acquired her, so I don't know what went into making her this way, but as a pet she was useless. I guess she ate and drank, but it was when no one else was around. She used the sandbox, too, because we never found any "accidents." Other than the vaccinations and worming I had given her the day she moved in, she had not received any veterinary care. I assume she stayed healthy, but I didn't know.

Okay, I was hurt. I was in a brace that held my leg straight, and I was on painkillers that didn't kill any pain. Spaced me out, yes, but I was spaced out in pain. I was also supposed to be on crutches, but they required a level of coordination I was unable to meet; I was probably safer without them.

Our bedroom is on the second floor. Ascending and descending the stairs was slow and painful, but I managed. Downstairs, all I could do was sit or lie on the couch and watch TV, but I could not get comfortable. I couldn't sit in a normal chair because my leg wouldn't bend, and there was just enough difference in height between the easy chair and the footstool to put a painful angle on my knee. Lying on the couch was only marginally better because the cushions were soft and didn't give enough support.

After the first couple of days of being grounded, in addition to being bored out of my mind, I found my knee would become increasingly painful as the day progressed. By evening it would be extremely painful, whereas in the morning it had only been very painful, so on the third or fourth day I climbed the stairs—slowly—and lay down on the bed for about half an hour. The support the mattress gave helped a lot to ease the discomfort.

That first time I went up, Gary zoomed out of the bedroom just as I entered it. Ditto the second day. Apparently she spent her days up there; rarely did anyone go to the second floor before mid-evening, so I guess she looked on it as a secure place to hang out.

After about four days of this, Gary's zoom slowed to a scurry. Whether she was getting accustomed to me appearing every day at about the same time—early afternoon—or realized that, with my lack of mobility, I was no threat to her, I don't know. It appeared that she spent her time on the bed, because in her reduced haste to leave, I had seen her jump off the bed as I entered the room.

One day after a couple of weeks of this, she didn't leave the bedroom. She scooted over to a corner of the room and lay there, but she kept her eyes on me. This continued for several days, but eventually, instead of eyeing me the entire time I was in the room, she went to sleep.

It was another couple of weeks before the next step. I limped into the room one day and she stayed on the bed. She was obviously very tense and was ready to run if necessary, but she stayed there. I lay down and she very cautiously moved as far from me as she could and still lie on the bed. She remained tense but didn't leave.

"It's okay, Gary," I said, "I'm not going to hurt you." She looked unconvinced.

47

This went on for several days. One day while I was lying there reading and Gary was on the far side of the bed (I thought), I felt something pushing against my foot. I put my book down and looked to see what it was.

Gary had moved over next to me and was rubbing her head against the side of my foot! I reached for her, slowly, but she moved away. The next day, she rubbed against my leg, but again withdrew when I tried to touch her. This went on every day—foot or leg—and I stopped trying to reach for her.

Then I fell asleep one day. I was awakened by Gary's head rubbing against my hand, and in a few more days she let me rub her in return. I told Barb about it, but I couldn't prove it because Gary ran whenever she came into the room.

Gary and I had become friends. She rubbed against me and I petted her, but only when we were alone together. She became more friendly every day, but when we went to bed for the night, she would disappear. One night—or I should say one morning—at about three A.M., I felt one of my hands being pushed against. It was Gary asking to be petted. I patted her a couple of times, and then something must have startled her because she jumped down and ran.

I was still pretty immobile and pretty appalled by much of daytime TV. My seat of choice for this displeasure was the living room couch, which was easily viewed from the stairs to the second floor. Late one morning, a few days after the middle-of-the-night episode, I was home alone. Our son was off at college and our daughter, now in high school, seemingly only came home to sleep. Barb was shopping and the dogs were outside, so everything was very quiet when I noticed some movement out of the corner of my eye. I looked over and saw Gary slinking down the stairs. At the bottom she stopped, tensed, and looked around, prepared to flee if necessary. When no danger was seen (or imagined), she made two great leaps and landed on the couch.

"Hi, Gary," I said. She stared at me. A minute later she moved next to me and rubbed her head on my hand. She lay there by me, letting me pet her for a long time, until the phone rang. She leaped up and tore back up the stairs to the sanctuary of the bedroom, where she stayed until I hobbled up an hour or so later. She lay by my side as I read.

The downstairs visits occurred often from then on, but only when no one else was home. She would also want to be petted most nights. Still, though, no one else was to be trusted.

One night a few weeks later, Barb was having difficulty falling asleep. She was lying there awake but not moving when Gary jumped on the bed. I was asleep, but Barb later told me that Gary began rubbing against my arm and Barb reached over and petted her. Gary sat still for it.

The next step in Gary's socialization occurred just before I was able to return to the real world. She had been making nightly bed hops for quite some time and letting Barb touch her (but not in the daytime), and Gary had actually appeared downstairs once or twice, albeit hurriedly, when someone other than me was there.

This particular night, Barb and I were awakened by a loud, deep, rumbling noise. Waking me is no great challenge—

I'm a very light sleeper—but waking Barb is a trick. I think she goes into a coma every night. But this woke her too.

And it got louder! And closer!

Then a cat head rubbed against my hand, and I realized what it was. Gary was purring! Up to this point in Gary's life, we had only heard one sound from her: a small hiss on the day I brought her home years before. No meows, no purrs, no nothing, ever.

Apparently years and years of suppressed purrs had finally come to the surface and were being loosed on us. Barb said the bed shook, but it probably didn't.

As time has gone on, the purring has subsided to a fairly normal level, but she still does it only in the middle of the night. Gary comes down more often and will sometimes visit me even if other people are in the room—she will not visit them. Too much commotion—a sigh, a weight shift, a leg crossing—will send her zipping off to safety.

She's still a long way from normal, but in middle age she has learned a little trust. I'm not sure love is what she feels for me, but I think she derives pleasure from my company and I know I enjoy hers. It makes the pain of the kick from Max's yearling worth it, although I don't plan to befriend any more cats in this manner.

Crossing
the Border

Sally Huxley

My paternal grandfather was an avid fisherman. By profession he was an attorney, but he put as much enthusiasm into catching speckled trout as he did into the practice of law.

In the late twenties, after hearing a fish tale from a reliable source, he drove twenty hours straight over bad roads to a lake, only to be told that in another lake six hours north of Toronto, the fish were bigger. "Prizefighters," he remembered the man saying.

The next year he lured Grandmother to the lake. The year after that he built a summer house—a fishing camp, he called it—on Kaminiskeg Lake. In Algonquin Indian, the name meant "the lake of the wild geese." Grandfather always thought it was a mistranslation and substituted the word "fish" for geese. Since roads had not reached that part of the lake, the only access then was by boat.

It was a time when big, sprawling houses were built. The design was a rectangle, with a central living room and bedrooms on either side. Grandfather swore he had made the blueprint on a paper bag, and the workmen

51

followed his architectural plan. Grandmother penciled in the amenities—indoor plumbing and a separate wing for their five boys.

I have spent part of every summer in that house since I was two. As a child I enjoyed hot weather, bathing suits, and noisy cousins. Now I prefer September, when the tourists have gone and the leaves are in color.

Although we had never traveled anywhere with our cat Pip, I could not imagine leaving him. My father-in-law had recently stayed with us, and Pip, in one of his more perverse moods, had waited until late at night to jump on his bed, walk across his stomach, and then jump down. He suggested that if we wanted to take Pip, or "that awful cat," as he called him, to Canada, we should consider leaving him there. He was convinced that Pip would ruin our vacation. I was equally convinced that I would miss Pip too much. Even though Pip had definite opinions about cars— he hated all of them—we decided that he should go with us to Canada.

Since the cottage was five hundred miles from home, backpacking was out of the question, especially when we considered what we were taking with us. Pip's baggage was substantial. Cat litter and litter box, scratching post, a bed cushion—our canopy bed where he usually slept was too large to put in the car—toys, and cases of his food.

I left him alone and went to count out his cans of food. I figured five cans a day to be safe.

"That's ridiculous," Bob said. "We couldn't even eat that

much a day." Since I was in charge of the cat food, I ignored
Bob and put in five cans a day, plus an extra week's supply. I
figured if my appetite increased dramatically in Canada, why
couldn't Pip's.

We loaded the car during one of Pip's naps, which gave
us ample time. Our car is a station wagon with an enormous
well that I filled immediately with essentials such as old *New
Yorkers*—Does anyone ever read them when they come?—
Russian novels, and things I want to keep but not in our house
in New Hope.

Dr. Tindall had left us knockout pills to calm Pip.
Hypothetically, Pip would be sound asleep two hours
after the pills were given. Since we already knew the ins and
outs of giving a cat a pill—you put it in, he spits it out—
we were wary.

We resorted to silly talk, hoping that we'd catch Pip off-
guard. "Take your medicine like a good boy," Bob said. A bad
Texas accent didn't fool Pip.

Finally, I used our foolproof method and ground the
pills up in his food. Pip had favorites, although they changed
whenever I bought cases on sale. I don't know how he knew,
but invariably he turned up his nose at anything I bought at
a discount.

Pip obviously hadn't seen the cases of savory salmon in
the cupboard, so he cooperated and ate. The way to undo a
cat is through his stomach, delicate or not. We waited for
Pip to fall asleep. Since he slept most of the morning
anyway, it was difficult to determine the effect of the pill

versus his natural state. He curled up on the chair. I tiptoed in and out of the room, checking on him.

I picked him up from the cushion on the chair and carried him to the car—so far, so good. I put my ear close to him to make certain he was breathing.

We decided a carrier would frighten him, so I put him down on his bed and closed the car door. Instantly, wide-eyed, yowling, he was awake. He reminded me of the cartoons where you see a cat's tail plugged into an outlet.

Only temporarily, we thought. After all, these were knockout pills. We tried telling him how lucky he was because most cats ride in small containers, and he had a whole station wagon to himself with two chauffeurs at his beck and call.

Bob tried to reassure him. He even sang a lullaby. We had treats and milk and a goose-down pillow and a vocalist. "Anything you want," Bob said. What Pip wanted was to get out and have Bob stop singing.

Pip yowled and caterwauled in unison with Bob. He hung from the roof of the car upside down. He managed to stay that way for the first ten miles, defying gravity. Finally he discovered he could make louder, more pitiful sounds if he stood on the back of the front seat and screeched into our ears. When the man at the turnpike entrance handed us our ticket and said, "Have a good day," we could hardly hear him. We were going deaf from the noise.

Pip meanwhile set up camp in the back on top of a dried flower arrangement I had made especially for the dining room table.

By mile one hundred, he had calmed down a little and set off to explore everything in the car, including the driver. He preferred the view from the brake pedal. It was one of the rare times he seemed to enjoy looking up, instead of down at us.

He stopped crooning by mile two hundred. He was awake and had started to use the back of the car as a race track. He shunned his bed and sat on top of his scratching post, assuming a loftier, more natural position. We thought he was relaxing. He was getting his second wind.

We stopped for gas at an out-of-the-way station in upstate New York. The sign off of I-81 seemed simple enough—*Gas This Way*. By the time we got to Al's Service, I was certain we would see bilingual signs welcoming us to Canada.

It was time to walk Pip. We had read a book on traveling with a cat. Obviously, it was ghostwritten. It was, as they say, a book that will live in infamy in the annals of bad advice: "It is helpful to walk your animal when you stop for gas. This will give them needed exercise and make them happy for the rest of the trip."

I took out the leash and hooked it to Pip's collar. I started off toward the bushes with Al staring at me. At first I thought it was because he valued his landscaping and did not want anything dropped beneath his brambles. I assured him with my eyes, and the help of a leaping cat, that I had no intention, and neither did Pip, of soiling his property. Pip was interested in the woods.

Pip trotted along, going under the prickly wild roses, and dragging me through them. He was out for revenge and had no intention of going back to the car.

Finally, I gave the leash a tug. Pip sat down and moved backwards. It was then I realized he was trying to be Houdini and get out of his collar. I scooped him up and hurried back to the car.

"Don't see that much," Al said.

I nodded.

"Walking a cat, I mean. Don't see that at all."

"He's trained," I said.

"I can see that." He looked at the burrs on my pant legs.

Pip was miffed. I unsnapped the leash, and put him in the back on his favorite box, which he now decided he hated. He stomped across my dried flower arrangement again and stared out the window as we drove away toward the border.

When we changed drivers, Pip changed his tactics from sullenness to an all-out attack. He slunk across the front seat and jumped on the floor.

Scratch! Scratch! He pulled his claws back and forth across the green carpet. Perhaps had we told him we hated its ugly color and didn't care, he might have stopped. Instead we ignored him. My mother always said that children did not like to play to an empty theater.

We soon found out that ignoring Pip worked to his advantage, not ours. Like the most practiced of abusers, he was out to leave a mark where it didn't show. He sat on my lap, purring, and began to use my jeans as a scratching post.

By the time we reached the border he was asleep.

"We're in Canada now. Look at the water. The Thousand Islands." Pip detested water in almost any form except the toilet bowl, and didn't open an eye. I kept remembering our family trips to Canada. After we had been driving an hour, my sisters and I would say, "Are we in Canada yet, Dad?" Pip's lack of enthusiasm for anything other than destruction should have forewarned us.

I had all the health documents in my hand. I pushed the button for my window and by mistake hit the large rear window.

"Where are you folks from?" the customs man asked.

"Pennsylvania," I answered as Bob said, "New York." We seemed to be just your average, estranged couple. "The States," we said, looking at each other. At least we agreed on that.

"Any building materials? Nails?"

We shook our heads. It was one of the few things that we weren't bringing into Canada.

"We have a cat," I said, and I handed him Pip's vaccination certificate, a sort of cat passport. The paper stated that Pip was a DSH (domestic shorthair), and that he had been vaccinated against everything except measles and car sickness.

"Where's the cat?" the man said.

I pointed to the back. No Pip. I pointed again.

He looked at me as if I were James Stewart traveling

with a large, white, invisible rabbit. He handed me back the papers and told us that he hoped we found our cat.

"We've lost him," I said to Bob. "We've lost Pip."

"How can we lose a cat in a car? He's under something. He couldn't get out,"

Then we remembered the open window.

I stopped the car and pulled over to the side where they examined the cars. I was prepared to unload everything. They'd see curtain rods and a case of wine and an electric grill—all contraband. But we hadn't lied. We truly didn't have any building materials.

Dr. Tindall had said that cats use a magnetic field to determine direction. Until they reorient themselves they could get lost. If Pip had escaped, he would be on his way back to Pennsylvania.

Just as I was about to rip the car apart, Pip resurfaced. He had been sleeping in a box filled with our lunch. This seemed to remind him he was hungry. I hadn't intended to feed him in the car. Having checked with the vet, I was certain Pip could survive nine hours without food. Bob and I couldn't.

Though ham was not Pip's favorite, he gave every indication that he would consider taking a bite. He jumped on my lap and put his paws against my chest and licked part of my sandwich. When I was growing up, and there was only one piece of pie left, my sister Ann would wet her fork with her tongue and put it on the pie, declaring the dessert hers.

Pip used a slightly modified, but effective technique.

I relinquished my sandwich to him more easily than he would have given up his Fancy Feast. He bit into the sandwich and spit it out—a culinary snob, not content with the simple things in life. Disgruntled, he went back to ransacking the car.

Though I was pretty sure Pip could not read, he sat on everything I had marked *fragile*. With a great flourish and a leap, he pounced on a box of crystal. He finally tired of somersaulting at mile 450. The last fifty miles we wondered how we were going to get him out of the car and into the house without him fleeing. We were determined to foil any escape plans.

"Do you hear that scratching?" Bob said. "It sounds as if he's digging."

As I turned around, two dried hydrangeas flew into the air. "I don't hear anything," I said, ignoring the sounds. I looked for Pip, who seemed to be hiding.

It was getting dark, and we knew that cats see better in the dark than we do. I kept hearing Dr. Tindall tell us to grab him by the scruff of the neck the way mother cats do. I have always wanted to tell Tindall that mother cats grab their babies with their teeth.

The scratching increased as we pulled off the main highway and onto a dirt road. It sounded as if Pip were trying to tunnel his way out before we reached the house.

When I was a child, my sisters and I used to fight over who would open the gate leading down to our house. Now there is only one post standing with a rusty hinge embedded in the wood. A long time ago our neighbor had cattle and horses, and if the gate were left open, we would find his farm in our backyard. Though we rigorously denied doing it, my sisters and I sometimes left the gate open.

Our parents wanted us to see nature up close— raccoons prying the lids off garbage cans, porcupines whittling the wood on our porch—but cows eating our grass were shooed away.

"Raccoons," I said to Bob. "There are raccoons up here."

"We have raccoons at home."

"But these are smarter, meaner," I said, remembering one surly raccoon that wanted a better grade of garbage. "If Pip gets loose and he meets a Canadian raccoon . . ."

"We could stay in the car for two weeks," Bob said.

Pip began to yowl as we turned into the driveway.

We decided that I would grab him and rush him into the house. Bob would hold open the door, an integral part of the plan.

"We have to be quick," Bob said, fumbling with the car door. "Everything's going to be fine."

I was not reassured. I was certain someone had said the same thing to Joan of Arc.

I grabbed Pip and headed for the door. I was reminded of that old story of what was behind the door, the lady or the tiger. What I could definitely say was that it was not Bob. He was at a different door. Screaming does not soothe a squirming cat, so I mildly yelled to Bob and asked him where he was. He finally opened the right door. Pip jumped down, took a swipe at my leg, and fled underneath the kitchen table to sulk.

I did not like the look on his face. He put his paws beneath his chin, elevating his glare. We knew it was only a matter of time before he exacted his revenge, but for now he would wait. Tomorrow was another day, and he had to get his sleep in order to outwit us.

A Cat Named
Sweetie

Richard H. Schneider

Perhaps my antagonism toward cats dated from the time I used to chase them from my father's fish pool with a garden hose. To me, cats were snooty creatures with an insouciant air of independence, not at all like good-hearted dogs, who slavered for attention and practically somersaulted for a pat on the head.

When my younger son, Kit, carried in a gray-and-white kitten he had found, I reluctantly accepted the new addition. Kit and his brother, Peter, named her Sweetie, and she soon made friends with our two dachshunds. But the cat and I were not close.

Everything changed when we moved to a small farm in northern Virginia, where Sweetie enjoyed roaming our barn and nearby field. One evening we returned from shopping to hear a plaintive cry from the barnyard. Out of the shadows came Sweetie, crawling on her belly. Kit picked her up and cried, "She's been hurt!"

Her lower legs were in bloody shreds. Evidently she had been bush-whacked by a sickle from someone mowing the adjacent field. We called a local veterinarian, who said to bring her by in the morning. "She'll be dead long before that," gasped my wife, Betty.

We called a friend, who suggested a big-animal vet in nearby Leesburg. Although the vet was tending a sick horse at the time, he said to bring our cat right over.

Kit drove while I held Sweetie on my lap, cushioning her on a towel. As the headlights cut through the black trees lining the small dirt road, I found myself talking to Sweetie, praying for her and gently rubbing between her shoulder blades with my thumb. That seemed to soothe her.

The vet, William Rokus, met us at the door of his office. He was a giant man dressed in khaki, with hands the size of hams. What could he do for our pitiful bundle of fur?

The man gently took Sweetie, gave her a shot that knocked her out, and then sat down to work while Kit and I watched. An aura of compassion emanated from the huge man as he worked ever so patiently and carefully, those big hands expertly wielding suture and needle as he deftly stitched Sweetie's shredded paws and legs. Finally he handed me the cat, gave us instructions and medication, and told us that he thought Sweetie just might make it.

We drove home in silence. The next morning we coddled Sweetie, fed her warm milk and stroked her fur. Again I found myself rubbing her between the shoulder blades, and she cocked her head to squint up at me.

In a few days Sweetie was clumping around on plaster casts and before long was limping on paws that looked remarkably normal, thanks to the skill of William Rokus.

Soon Sweetie was patrolling the barn again, but she never returned to the field. When an engine started up, she streaked from sight. She always had a slight limp, but it never seemed to bother her. When we moved to New York she became a city cat, reigning over her yard and hissing off any creature that had the audacity to edge close.

But some kind of bond had been struck between Sweetie and me that night. When I read the paper or worked at my typewriter, a warm bundle of fur sprang into my lap to rest and purr. At night she curled on my pillow against my head.

Sweetie lived for sixteen years, quite old for a cat. It has been a few years since she died peacefully in her sleep, but I still think of her. She taught me so much.

I learned that we should avoid prejudice, that we should not judge proficiency by appearance, and that God does listen to our prayers for animals.

I also discovered that everyone has a need when wounded, whether it's for quiet companionship, a sympathetic word, or a gentle massage between the shoulder blades.

A Contrary Nature

Jaqueline Damian

I've lived with cats so long that I tend to take their contrarian nature for granted. It's just part of what is, like air. But a friend who just got his first kitten doesn't quite know what to make of her. This little beige tiger, rescued off the street at roughly three weeks old, gives him mixed messages.

"If I've been away," says my friend, "the cat is so ecstatic to see me that she throws herself at my feet, rolls around on her back, waves her paws in the air, and chirps. But once I've been home for a while, she ignores me. She runs around and plays, and won't have anything to do with me—unless she's in the mood, of course."

This kitten has deeply bonded with my friend, who had to feed her with an eyedropper when he first brought her home because she was too little to know how to eat or drink on her own. It's not indifference, or lack of love, that causes her to scamper off when he makes a grab for her. It's something deep in the nature of the beast.

Perhaps the crux of the matter lies in the symbol of the straight line. This is a geometry, as Vicki Hearne points out in her book *Adam's Task: Calling Animals by Name*, that cats seem to scorn. Just as there are no straight lines in nature, so there are none in a cat's world.

Consider, for example, Sasha's typical trajectory when he comes inside for dinner: In the front door with a diagonal swing over to the telephone stand, which he rubs with his right cheek to mark proprietarily via glands near the mouth and on the forehead, with scent too subtle for human detection; a leap onto the counter that separates kitchen from living room, followed by a leap onto the antique pie safe opposite it and another to the kitchen workstation where I am scooping out the cat food. Then down to his food dish to eat.

This route is not the shortest distance between two points. It lacks Euclidean elegance and is needlessly convoluted, unless one subscribes to the ancient Chinese belief that devils fly in straight lines.

Similarly, when I stood at the front door tonight and called for Sasha to come in, he didn't make a beeline for home. Rather, he sprinted toward me down the gravel path in front of the house, skidded to a stop midway to sniff at a patch of grass that caught his attention, then raced forward again—and again stopped short to investigate something else. Finally he crossed through the garden, angled over to the fieldstone walkway leading to the door, and marched inside.

I stood there and waited, since I know from experience that if I should hie over and pick the cat up intending to carry him inside, he would struggle out of my arms and stalk regally toward the door, nicking his bushy black tail expressively to signal his annoyance.

If cats are sometimes mystifying, it's because they prefer the indirect to the direct, the oblique to the straightforward, the parabola to the straight line. It's as if, in bringing cats into our homes, we are introduced to a culture as intricate and riddled with taboos as any described in the anthropology texts—and where it's just as easy to give offense.

Say I am sitting on the couch reading or watching TV and Sasha wants to cuddle up with me. Never, ever will he leap directly onto my lap. First he walks back and forth in front of the couch and jumps on and off the coffee table a few times until he is sure he has my attention, staring at me intently all the while. After a moment, I catch on to the fact that I am being given my cue. I'm supposed to lie down on the couch, flat on my back (Sasha doesn't like being a lap cat; he prefers a reclining human), and drape the woolen throw that hangs from the arm of the couch over my chest and stomach. Then and only then will Sasha jump on me and begin the intensive front-paw kneading that precedes his settling down for a snooze. (Does he insist on the throw to protect me from his claws as he kneads?)

If I make a grab for him before the ritual backing and forthing has been fully played out, he squirms away and repeats the whole ceremony, circling around, jumping on and off the coffee table, and staring, this time with a hint of reproach in his eyes. Clearly, the decision to cuddle, and its timing, must be his and his alone; I cannot impose it on him or hurry it along.

Sometimes my untoward attempt at direct action so offends him that he ostentatiously marches to the front door as if he wants to go outside, casting a meaningful glance back over his shoulder. Since I know he does not, in fact, want to go out but wants instead to cuddle, I am chastened into lying down again, shawl in place, and passively awaiting his decision to circle in for another approach. Having made his point, he soon does.

Killer Cat

Arnetta Baugh

I was four years old the warm spring day my little sister was born. I spent the day on the farm with my grandmother. That same morning, Grandma's big gray tabby gave birth to four kittens—two black-and-white ones, one gray marbled one, and the last one yellow-and-white striped.

"Do you think I can have the yellow striped one, Grandma? He's so cute."

"We'll have to ask your mom when she gets home from the hospital, Lindy."

Grandma lived on the farm next to ours, so every day I walked to her house to play with the kittens and watch them grow. When the kittens were weaned, I brought the tiny yellow one home and named him Tom-Cat.

Mother reminded me, "No animals in this house, not even a kitten cute as this. You can keep him on the back porch. I put a box out there for him to sleep in. I have baby Sarah to take care of, Lindy, so you'll have all the responsibility for its care."

"I will, I promise, Mama, I will. I'll take good care of him."

I tiptoed into the house, past the sleeping baby, to find my favorite doll blanket, the one with teddy bears on it, and tucked it in the box. Three or four times a day, I carried out a bowl of warm milk and some table scraps for him.

After I started kindergarten, Tom-Cat became so lonesome he took up with the chickens. He slept with them at night, often scaring away the skunks that came there looking for eggs. He never killed any of the robins or sparrows that nested in our apple trees. He was, however, good at catching mice. He would play with them, toss them in the air, let them go, and tackle them again and again; finally, by the tail, he would drag them under the porch out of sight.

Tom-Cat let me carry him around for hours. His lanky body hung out both below and above my arms. When he decided he'd had enough of my play, he'd lick my hands and face with his sandpaper tongue, making me weak with laughter. I could never ride my favorite Appaloosa, Blossom, without Tom-Cat pressed between the saddle horn and me.

I gave up playing with dolls, because I had Tom-Cat to dress up in my doll clothes, complete with bonnet, sweater, and socks. I'd put him in my doll buggy and away we'd go.

"Ooh, Tom-Cat," I'd croon to him as he lay back on the pillows and blankets. "You look so cute all dressed up. You really are my baby, aren't you?"

One Saturday afternoon in August when I was seven, two of my friends and I were running through the sprinklers when mean old Mr. Larsen came rushing into our front yard yelling, "I'm gonna kill that cat of yours. Been eatin' my chickens. Scatterin' feathers everywhere."

I ran into the house. "Daddy, Daddy, come quick. Stinky old Mr. Larsen's out here and says he's gonna kill Tom-Cat."

My father jumped up from the table where he was reading the newspaper. "No one's goin' to kill Tom-Cat, Lindy." He pushed up his shirtsleeves past his elbows and charged out the door. "What's this all about, Fred?"

"Your cat killed some of my chickens."

"That's not possible, and I'll show you why."

Daddy hugged me and held my hand as we walked toward the chicken coop. Mr. Larsen followed us into the backyard, into the cool of the shaded chicken coop. Just as my father expected, there, sound asleep, was my precious cat all snuggled in a nest with one of our chickens. Daddy reached for Tom-Cat and scratched his ears, waking him. Tom-Cat stretched, jumped out of the nest and came over to me. I picked him up and gathered him in my arms.

Mr. Larsen hung his head, laughing. "I guess you're right, Ray. That can't be the cat I saw. This cat's a chicken lover."

As Dad and Mr. Larsen strolled away from the coop, Mr. Larsen slapped my dad on the back. "Where'd you ever find a killer cat like that there?"

"I knew you couldn't hurt any of them chickens, Tom-Cat." I hugged my best buddy. He gazed up at me with his large green eyes, purring contentedly.

Make Up
Your Mind!

Arthur Gordon

This morning our big cat, Oreo (so named because he is a handsome black-and-white), and I went through our familiar ritual at the back door. Oreo had been outside for a while and he really wanted to come in. So I opened the door and waited. I thought ruefully of the Bible passage: "Behold, I stand at the door . . ." But would he come in?

No, he wouldn't. He stopped and lowered his head suspiciously, as if I were some deadly enemy. "Come on, Oreo," I said, tapping my foot impatiently.

He sat thoughtfully and began to wash his face with one paw. Maddening.

"Oreo," I said, "I give you food. I supply all your needs. If you do anything in return, I don't know what it is. Now I'm personally inviting you into my house. So come on in!"

Oreo put one foot across the threshold, then drew it back. He looked out across the yard with some remote, unfathomable expression. He still wouldn't come into the house.

"Oreo," I said, "I'm not going to stand here forever. If you don't come in, I'm going to close this door. This is your last chance!"

Slowly I started to close the door. Did he come in? No, he sat there, exercising his free will or something. He'll come when it suits him, not before. He figures I'll be patient. So far, he's right.

God made cats. He also made people. I wonder how God feels, sometimes, when he stands at the door and waits . . . and waits . . .

I think I know.

Help and Healing

from Unlikely Heroes

Kitten in
the Toolshed

Katherine Yurchak

S tanding beside the kitchen window to catch a small breeze that summer day in 1991, I heard faint sounds coming from the direction of my husband's toolshed out back. *Did Nick decide to give work a try again?* My spirits leapt for a moment and then quickly plummeted when I stepped into the living room. Nick was sitting on the sofa, his whole demeanor listless and defeated. He had been like that since the stroke he had suffered about two years earlier. He did not even look up from his newspaper as I walked past and went outside to investigate. A doleful wail sent me hurrying to the shed. *Goodness, that sounds like a baby crying for its mother!* I thought, tugging at the door. It opened with a reluctant creak. I saw that my guess hadn't been far off. On the floor by the workbench lay a tiny kitten struggling to separate itself from the lifeless bodies of its four siblings.

I knelt and carefully picked up the kitten. What a wee puff of yellow fur she was; she hardly filled the palm of my hand. I cradled the trembling creature close to me and carried her into the house.

"Look what I found in the shed," I said to my husband.

"Something must have happened to her mother." Nick didn't say a word, but at least he didn't look away when I sat down in the rocking chair with the tiny kitten. I asked him, "How are we going to keep this little thing alive?"

"You should've left the animal where you found it," came Nick's blunt reply. He shook his head and slowly dragged himself from the sofa. "I'm going to my doctor's appointment," he announced.

I watched as Nick shuffled out of the room. I wished there were something that I could do to help him. The doctors had yet to find a way to ease the lingering effects of my husband's stroke—the stiffness in his right shoulder and the pain that wracked his right arm. Every night I massaged his arm and pressed warm, wet towels on his shoulder, but the pain wouldn't go away.

Nor, it seemed, would the malaise that shadowed Nick's soul, no matter how much I encouraged him. The stroke had abruptly ended the work that he loved. It was this blow I was beginning to fear he would never recover from.

For thirty years my husband had been a self-employed electrician and master mechanic. People for miles around knew there wasn't anything Nick couldn't fix. Our phone was always ringing with folks asking for help with one broken-down thing or another. "Don't worry, I'll take care of it," Nick would assure them, scanning his list of service calls to be made. He'd whistle when he left for work in the morning. And how I loved to listen for his whistling as he walked back to the house after putting his tools away in the shed at day's end.

The stroke had changed all that. Nick could no longer wield his tools for any length of time, and I'd had to tell callers, "Sorry, he's not able to help you right now." I'd tried to convince Nick his strength and his work would come back to him, but the weakness in his right side hadn't improved. Eventually the phone had fallen silent. So, too, had Nick's whistling. His tools lay gathering dust in the shed, abandoned, just like I knew Nick felt, even though he wasn't the kind to talk about his feelings.

Lord, it breaks my heart to see Nick closed in on himself like this, I prayed. *I've done all I can. Can't you please help him— us—get through this?*

"Mee-ew . . . mee-ew." The kitten's cries sounded weaker. I looked into her scrunched-up face and told her, "Well, at least I can do something to help you." We'd never had pets, but I figured what this kitten needed couldn't be all that different from what our grown son had needed when he was a baby.

What could I use to get the kitten to nurse? Ah, the small plastic bottle I'd been saving for oiling my sewing machine. And something soft so she'd feel like she was at her mother's breast. "It's okay, lunch is coming," I said to the kitten as I went out to Nick's shed again. I grabbed a piece of rubber tubing and shut the door, trying not to look at the lonely tools lying on the workbench.

Back in the house, I filled the bottle with warm milk and fitted the tubing on the spout. I wrapped the kitten in a scrap of flannel I dug out of my sewing basket, then held her close to me and settled in the rocking chair. "Here you are, little one," I said, touching the bottle's soft rubber tip to her quivering pink nose. Her instincts took over and soon she dozed off, her belly full of milk.

Not an hour later she woke and hollered for more. "You sure know what you need, don't you?" I said with a laugh.

She was napping again when Nick came back from his appointment. I couldn't believe the first words out of his mouth. "How's the kitten?" he asked.

"I think she just might make it."

"That's good," he said, "because the mother won't be coming back." He explained that on his way home, he'd seen a large yellow cat lying dead on the road.

Just then the kitten spoke up again, loud and clear. "Mee-ow . . . mee-ow!"

"Why don't you feed her?" I said to Nick, handing him the tiny, flannel-swaddled bundle before he could say no.

He sat down in the rocker, and the kitten nestled into the crook of his right arm. As soon as he offered the bottle, she began guzzling frantically. "Since you seem so determined to stick around," Nick said to her, "I suppose we're going to have to give you a name." He looked to me, chuckling. "What do you think?"

What I thought was that I was so glad to hear my husband taking a bit of joy in life again that I wanted to put my hands together right there and give thanks to God. Not wanting to make a big deal out of it, though, I said simply, "She sure has a nice, strong holler. How about naming this kitten Holly?"

The corners of my husband's mouth crinkled up. "Hi, Holly," he said, touching a finger to the kitten's nose.

After that, Nick was no longer at a loss for what to do—not when there was a lively and curious kitten to keep up with. I don't know who was following whom, really, because Holly, for her part, wouldn't let my husband out of sight for long. She'd lie beside him while he napped in the afternoon. When we turned in at night, Holly would jump onto our bed, pad her way across Nick's pillow, and cuddle up right against his shoulder. That's where we'd find her when we woke, her big amber eyes blinking good morning. Even after Holly graduated to eating cat food (plus her favorite tuna) out of a dish and no longer needed to be bottle-fed, she still liked to snuggle in the crook of Nick's arm. I couldn't help thinking that carrying the kitten, ball of fluff though she was, was building up Nick's strength.

One nippy September evening, a friend stopped by to collect donations for our town's volunteer fire department. While I was rummaging for my purse, Holly slipped out the open door.

"Holly! Holl-eee!" Nick and I called until our voices were hoarse. With flashlights, we searched every corner of the yard, praying all the while. What would Nick do without Holly?

Shivering in the autumn night, I finally had to abandon the search. I sat alone in the kitchen, hoping against hope that Nick would burst in with Holly cradled in his arms. The door opened and I jumped up. But the look on Nick's face made me slump back into my seat. "Better give up," he muttered.

I couldn't bear to see defeat in his eyes again, not after he'd come so far. As I turned away, I saw the dish on the kitchen floor. Why hadn't we thought of it? Quickly I spooned tuna from a can. Nick opened the door and I stood in the doorway. Tapping the spoon against the dish, I called, "Holly! Tuna, Holly!"

Like lightning, a golden streak zipped through the door.

Then, dinner devoured, Holly looked up at us, her amber gaze steady, as if nothing at all had happened.

But I knew something had changed when I heard Nick say unabashedly, "Thank you, Lord, for bringing Holly back. And for sending this little creature to comfort us in the first place." Who would ever have thought my stoic husband would be praying over a kitten?

That surprise was nothing compared to what I witnessed the following spring. By that time Holly had become a full-grown cat with claws that were turning our upholstery to tatters. "We're not going to have anywhere to sit if she keeps this up," I complained to Nick one morning as I shooed Holly from the already-shredded corner of the sofa.

"Don't worry, I'll take care of it," he said. Before I could ask what he meant, he scooped up Holly and went out.

I watched them from the kitchen window. Nick strode purposefully—straight to the toolshed!

For the first time since his stroke, I saw Nick slowly creak the shed door open. I held my breath as he stepped inside with the cat. Then the door swung shut behind them, and I could only wonder at what they were doing.

I was almost done sewing a patch on the tattered sofa when I heard a faint whistling getting nearer and stronger. Could it be? I flung open the door.

Nick stood there beaming, holding Holly in the crook of his right arm and a homemade cat tree in his left hand. It was just a few pieces of wood hammered together and covered with remnants of rugs, but to me, it was my husband's greatest masterpiece.

Nick returned to his toolshed with Holly the next day. And every day after that. Before long our neighbors noticed he was back at his workbench, and the calls started coming in again.

Nine years later, at age eighty, Nick still isn't ready to retire. Nearly every day he's out in the shed, putting his tools to good use—all under the watchful gaze of a certain marmalade-yellow cat, who has her own seat at the workbench, not far from where I found her. Or, rather, where I was led to her. After all, looking at how perfectly this orphaned kitten fit into our lives, I have to say there is nothing the good Lord can't take care of once we ask him to put his hand to it.

Herbie's Purr

Ruth McDaniel

S*cratch, scratch . . .*

I looked up from the insurance form I was trying to fill out and glanced toward the kitchen. *Could that be what I thought it was? No, that's impossible.* It sounded just like a paw softly scratching the screen door—something I hadn't heard since Fluffy, our cat of twenty years, had died.

Fluffy had wandered into our lives, a stray. "She looks like she's been living off the land for a while now," my husband, W.T., said as we watched her stealthily creep along the border of our backyard early one evening. She was clearly looking for food, but the second we opened the door she shot back into the woods.

"The poor thing," I said as the cat peeked out at us from among the leaves. "She's afraid of people. Too wary for her own good."

"She'll come around," W.T. said. "She just needs some time to learn to trust us."

Every evening when he got home from work, W.T. went straight out back with a bowl of milk or food. Finally the day came when he was able to stroke the cat's yellow fur once before she scampered back to the safety of the woods. "She's so fluffy!" he marveled. So that was how Fluffy came to have her name. For the next twenty years, though she was a beloved pet, she always retained that little spark of wildness and independence.

When Fluffy passed away, W.T. was heartbroken. It was a few months afterward that his own health began to decline. Now W.T. was gone, too, and I was alone in a house that had seemed wonderfully secluded when we'd moved in years back, but suddenly felt just plain lonely. And it had only been a week.

Scratch, scratch . . .

There it is again! Must be a branch rubbing against the window screen.

With W.T. gone, the sensible thing would have been to sell the house and move into a smaller space—one where the nearest neighbor wasn't a mile away. But there were no apartments in town, and I hated the idea of leaving the place where my husband and I had spent so many wonderful years. Plus there were all of W.T.'s possessions to deal with, from his tools and fishing gear to the little outboard he kept on blocks in the carport. Everywhere I looked there seemed to be another detail to worry about, and another reminder of my grief. *Lord, who is going to help me with all this? How will I get by?*

Scratch, scratch . . .

Okay, I've got to go see what that noise is. I put the insurance form down and went to the kitchen. I gave a little start when I saw the cat looking at me from behind the screen. *It can't be—but it looks just like Fluffy!* I pushed open the door, and my visitor, purring loudly, strolled right inside and rubbed against my leg. The yellowish color was the same as Fluffy's, but this cat was bigger—clearly a male—and a lot more trusting. Even after twenty years with us, Fluffy would never have just sauntered in like that.

All that thick fur couldn't conceal the cat's emaciated condition, and his meows begged for food. I poured a big bowl of milk, and the cat followed me out to the carport. He lapped up the milk eagerly. I spread out an old blanket in case he decided to stay for the night.

The next morning I called some neighbors and the town veterinarian, asking if anyone had lost a cat. No one had. I plunged into another day of bills, forms, and phone calls. In the afternoon, depressed and hardly able to think straight, I went into the kitchen to make myself a cup of coffee.

Scratch, scratch . . . There was that paw on the screen again.

"I guess you've got yourself a new owner," I said, opening a can of Fluffy's cat food I'd unearthed from the back of the cupboard. I served my new friend and sat down at the kitchen table to watch him eat. When he finished, he came over and hopped in my lap.

"You really are a friendly one! Herbie sounds like a good name for you," I said as I stroked his thick coat. Herbie set to purring that purr of his. Before I knew it, I began to feel like my old self again and even found the energy for a few more phone calls.

From then on, Herbie and I established a routine. Whenever some new bill or legal detail got the better of me, I'd go out back and holler, "Herbie!" There would be a rustle in the woods, and he'd run into the house, hop up onto my lap, and start purring. "Relax," the sound always seemed to say. "Things will work out. Just wait and see."

Herbie wasn't the only one giving me encouragement. When a storm blew some heavy branches down into the yard, a few friends from church showed up without my even asking and helped me clear them. One neighbor found a buyer for W.T.'s fishing boat, and another guided me through the confusing details of his insurance papers.

One morning, as I was reading the paper with Herbie curled contentedly in my lap, a friend called to tell me about a condominium that was going up in town. I could move to a more manageable space without leaving the area behind after all. I soon found a buyer for the house, and he agreed to take most of the furniture too. I also discovered that one of the neighbors who had helped me was an avid fisherman. It was a joy to be able to pass on W.T.'s gear to him. "See?" Herbie's purr seemed to say. "I told you so."

But as moving day approached, I found myself with a new worry. Herbie was an outdoor cat. Would he be comfortable in a small apartment? The last thing I wanted was to make him miserable by cooping him up. Like I always did now when a worry was starting to get the better of me, I went to the kitchen door.

"Herbie! Herrrrbie!"

But for the first time since that big yellow cat had walked into my life, Herbie was nowhere to be seen.

I drove around the countryside and made some calls—to no avail. Worried though I was, I somehow knew no harm had come to Herbie. When the time was right, he had left just as mysteriously as he had come. I said a prayer for his well-being and promised that when things got tough in the future, I'd remember that soothing purr of his. When I'd really needed it, God's help had been there—right at my screen door.

"He's My Cat, Mom"

Betty R. Graham

O ne Friday morning a few months ago, I had just walked into my office when the phone rang. I reached for it and heard my son's panicky voice: "Mom, you've gotta come home quick—Bootsie's been hit by a car!" I drove home promptly, worrying about Brian. His cat meant a lot to him.

We rushed Bootsie to the Mount Vernon Animal Hospital and waited anxiously while the veterinarian's expert fingers gently probed the animal's limp body. Then she ordered x-rays. I knew the prognosis was bad when she called me aside in the hall. "I'm afraid that he doesn't have much of a chance," she whispered.

I swallowed hard. "Well, do what is necessary, Doctor. Don't let him suffer." I didn't know how I was going to tell my son.

When we entered the examining room again, Brian turned his tearstained face to the doctor. "He will get better, won't he?" Fourteen-year-old boys aren't supposed to cry. I could see how he was struggling with his emotions and trying to act like a man. But the fear in his eyes belied his attempt at optimism.

"We'll do all we can, son," Dr. Prescott answered. "I'll have to keep him here awhile."

"We can come to see him, can't we?" Brian asked eagerly.

I'd never heard of visiting hours for cats, but the vet nodded. Did that mean that she wasn't going to put Bootsie out of his misery? I didn't ask.

In the car I tried to prepare Brian for the inevitable. We didn't seem to have much luck with pets. In the four years we had lived in Mount Vernon, Virginia, we had lost our little ten-year-old Yorkshire terrier, Timmy, and three other cats. Brian would get over the loss of one-year-old Bootsie, I told myself. After all, it was only a cat, and not a very affectionate one at that. He would all but knock me down to get at his food bowl, but once his fat tummy was filled, he ignored me. I could stand on the front porch and call him again and again, and he would turn his back and go the other way.

"We'll get another cat right away," I said to Brian.

"But I don't want another one, Mom," he sobbed, giving in to the worry inside him. "I want Bootsie. He's my cat."

Like every mother, I have times in my life when I wish I had the power to grant the impossible dreams of my children. Even though I know that disappointments help youngsters build the character and maturity needed to face adult life, I find it harder to deal with my boys' pain than with my own. At that moment, I would have given anything for a magic wand to wave over Bootsie. I wanted to be able to say, "Mommy fixed it, honey," as I had so often when Brian was growing up.

We drove to school, and I explained to the principal why Brian was late, asking that the teachers be a little understanding that day if he didn't concentrate fully on his studies. Then I returned to my office and dug into normal duties.

When I got home that afternoon, Brian met me at the door. "Can we go see Bootsie now?" he begged.

"Not today, Brian," I answered. "Dr. Prescott said we should wait until after the weekend." I changed the subject and started to prepare dinner.

I fixed Brian's favorite rice, and we played a game together after supper, but it was earlier than usual when Brian kissed me good-night. "Bootsie's got to be okay." he said. My heart ached for the child.

I went to bed too. Lying there, trying to sleep, I heard sounds in Brian's bedroom. Thinking that he was crying again, I quietly went to comfort him. Moonlight shone through the windows of his room and, peeping in, I could see Brian's dark silhouette. He was on his knees beside the bed, his hands folded, whispering a prayer. ". . . and he never did anything bad to anybody. Please, God, I know you can do it."

Aside from our daily grace at the table, I had not heard Brian speak aloud to God since the bedtime prayers we said together when he was small. When he reached his teens, his faith had become private.

I tiptoed back into my room, feeling ashamed. Not

once that day had I suggested that God might help. I call myself Christian and try to set an example for my children, yet I had not even thought of praying for a cat. But Brian had.

And why shouldn't he? Didn't God create all life and isn't it precious in his sight? If it were not so, why would he direct Noah to save the animals?

I had looked at the odds and had given up immediately. But inside the heart of my loving son, there was a spark of hope—and the childlike wisdom to know where to go for help. I knelt quietly beside my own bed and joined Brian in his petition.

On Monday morning I called Dr. Prescott. The veterinarian said that it wouldn't hurt if Brian came to visit his cat. "Bootsie's still alive," she told me, "but he won't eat. His chances are even slimmer if he doesn't take some nourishment. He won't have enough strength to get well."

Had the cat, too, given up?

That afternoon we went to the kennel area of the pet hospital. Dogs barked and cats meowed as we passed the metal cages. We found Bootsie stretched on his side, his eyes dull and glazed, his breathing labored. A portion of fur had been clipped from one hip, where the car had struck him. The cat's broken pelvis and ribs would heal, the vet told us, but other internal injuries caused more serious problems.

"Hey, Bootsie," Brian called softly. "How're ya doin', baby?" He gently stroked the sleek head, and the cat's tail twitched slightly. "You're gonna get better, Boots. I know you are!" Brian said confidently. "We love you."

The cat could not lift his head, though he opened and closed his eyes occasionally during the ten or fifteen minutes Brian stroked him and talked to him.

When we returned the next afternoon, Bootsie raised his head as Brian approached the cage, but his food remained untouched. Brian held the water bowl to Bootsie's lips, and the cat lapped a few times. Then Brian picked up the food bowl and offered a few crumbs on his fingers. The cat licked them off. A soft buzzing sound, an erratic purr, came from his throat.

The following afternoon, Boots was curled in his normal ball when we opened the cage door. His green eyes, now clear and shining, looked up at my son with nothing less than adoration. The cat had eaten some of the food in his bowl, and with Brian's help he finished his meal. My son's joy reached new bounds when Boots struggled to stand so that he could rub his cheek against Brian's hand.

Four more days went by before we were allowed to bring Bootsie home. He limped badly, and I thought he would be crippled for the remainder of his nine lives. But today you'd never guess that the cat had been hurt. He's once again fat and sleek. He runs as fast and jumps as high as he ever did. The only difference I see in that cat is his undisguised devotion to my son. When Brian comes home, Bootsie runs over, stands up on his now-strong hind legs, and greets Brian with a "kiss."

My neighbor Pam expressed my own feeling on the day we brought Bootsie home from the hospital. "It was love that saved that cat," she said. "Love can work miracles."

Yes, it was love—the pure love of a young boy with faith, who cared enough to communicate his feelings to his pet. But more, it was the perfect love of God, who hears every sincere prayer.

I had wished for a flimsy magic wand. My son reached out for the greatest power in the universe—the power of God's love for us all.

Cats, Dogs,
and Mr. Bean

Elaine Bosler

W hen I saw Mr. Bean step out of his car and head for our veterinary office carrying a basket, I wanted to hide. Not again! Edmund Bean had been bringing us kittens for the past year and a half. He had seven cats at home, three or four of them female—and since a cat can have three litters a year, he was an all-too-frequent visitor. He brought the kittens in on the pretext of having them put to sleep, but he knew that I couldn't bear to see this happen. I took them and tried to find homes for them.

"How can you do this, Mr. Bean?" I scolded. "By not spaying or neutering your cats, you're responsible for bringing unwanted animals into the world. Do you realize that in six years two breeding cats can have seventy-three thousand descendants? Just try to find homes for them."

"But you're talking about surgery," Mr. Bean whined, his breath coming in short gasps, "and sometimes cats die during surgery."

His mixed-up logic infuriated me. Biting my tongue, I snatched the basket of kittens from him and stormed to the back of the clinic. Six pairs of curious eyes peered up at me.

The cats' meows melted my heart, and I prepared to take them to my three-room house in Princeton, which I shared with thirty-seven dogs and thirty—make that thirty-six—cats.

But these new additions were the least of my troubles. As Princeton's dog officer, I had been fighting an ongoing battle with the town's selectmen. They claimed I took in too many strays, and that my boarding capacity was legally limited to ten dogs—forget the cats. Any additional dog staying with me longer than ten days had to be destroyed.

Maybe the reason I kept them anyway was that I was something of a stray myself. After several years of being a battered wife, I had finally got a divorce and found my calling: taking care of unwanted dogs and cats, most of which had also been abused. I guess God knew what I needed.

Homeless animals came to me from everywhere. Some were even thrown over the fence into my backyard. I nursed them, had them spayed or neutered, and then tried to find them homes.

By the fall of 1975 those thirty-seven dogs and thirty-six cats got me in a peck of trouble. A new neighbor complained to the town. Pressured, the selectmen issued an order: Get rid of those twenty-seven extra dogs. The controversy was picked up by the local news, and as a result, I lost my part-time job with the veterinarian.

Then who should show up at my house with another litter of kittens? Mr. Bean, of course. This time I was ready to give him a real tongue-lashing. But before I had a chance, he looked around my yard, saw the dogs lolling happily, and the cats stretching and yawning in the sun. He turned to me, his blue eyes full of hope: "Can I come and visit them?" What could I say?

So every week he came with a chicken roll. Sitting on a stump, he broke off pieces and fed all the cats. Somehow, seeing his love of animals—misguided as he was—began to soften my heart.

He told me he slaved all his life for low wages in a shoe factory. Never married, he lived alone in a small apartment. His cats were his family. Each night they gathered at the door to welcome him home. They snoozed in his lap while he watched television. "And they curl up around me when I go to sleep," he said, smiling wistfully. I began to understand why Jesus told us to stop judging by mere appearances (John 7:24), for the more I got to know Mr. Bean, the more I learned to love him. He really was a kind man.

Finally, the Princeton authorities told me I had ten days to get rid of my extra dogs. What was I to do? Which dogs could I eliminate? Dutchess, the German shepherd who lay at my feet? Two years earlier a gang of drunken teenagers had poured lighter fluid all over her and set her on fire. A horrified onlooker called me, and I rescued the dog. I shaved off the fur over her raw, burned parts, applied ointment, and nursed her back to health. Now she wouldn't leave my side.

What about Yo-Yo, my mongrel who bounced around happily but never barked? Her vocal cords had been removed at a medical laboratory to prevent her howling while being used for research. Or Nubar? Someone found him limping along Route 146 and brought him here. It cost me $450 to repair his shattered front leg. But his twelve years of friendship was worth it.

Knowing no other course to pursue, I turned to the only one I was sure could help: God, who had given me this calling. "Oh, Father," I prayed, "You know what these animals need. I'm doing my best with what you've given me. Please help me find them homes."

Then I thought of a piece of land I had seen in Barre, a town about fifteen miles away. The property was secluded; there would be no one around to complain. The problem was money; I had only enough to feed myself and my dogs and cats, and pay their vet bills. If I could just get enough to buy the land, I would sell my house and build a facility on it.

A few days later Mr. Bean came for a visit. "I've got something to talk over with you," he wheezed. Inside the house, I shooed four dogs off the couch and invited him to sit down.

"Miss Bosler," he said, "I've been doing a lot of thinking. It's wonderful what you're doing with these animals. And I know you're having trouble."

He shifted on the couch and drew a breath. "Well, the doctors give me a year to live. I have emphysema and an enlarged heart." He went on talking as if what he was about to say wasn't important at all: "It has taken me all my life to save eight thousand dollars. I'm going to give you six thousand and save the other two thousand to have myself buried. I just want to know that all these"—he waved a hand around the room—"have a place to live."

For a moment I stared at the thin little man who for months had been the butt of my scolding and complaining. This was not the way I had expected God to help me. I went over and hugged Mr. Bean. I'd never seen him so happy.

Mr. Bean's gift helped me start the Bosler Humane Society, the largest no-kill shelter in New England. The dogs sleep on their own blankets, freshly washed every day, and they have supervised recreation and eating periods. Groups of fifteen cats live in a dozen individual "homes." All animals are spayed or neutered, and checked to make sure they are healthy.

When I look back, I'm amazed. To date we've been able to save and find homes for more than nine thousand spayed or neutered animals. And all because of Mr. Bean, the man who couldn't help loving animals—and who became the answer to a prayer.

Jasper, Yoda, and Jesus

Margie Nadine Walker

I silently prayed for wisdom as I watched my twelve-year-old daughter, Kris, print these words on a large cardboard sign: *Lost—Black Kitten—Named "Yoda"—$10 Reward.* For the past four days after school, we had canvassed the neighborhood door to door, posted signs, and placed a "lost kitten" ad in the paper. Then, hoping to catch a glimpse of him, we walked and drove up and down the surrounding streets. But Yoda had disappeared.

From the very beginning, as soon as we discovered he was gone, we had prayed for Yoda. Now, as our little girl began to realize that we probably would never see him again, I yearned to find reassuring words to tell her. "Please, God," I prayed, "don't let her faith in you be shattered because of this. What can I say to her if we can't find her kitten?"

Our family's adventure with cats had started two years earlier, when we—yes, we—were adopted by a large, older, gray-striped cat, whom we named Jasper. He was "king" of the backyard, very dignified, and for the past two years he had reigned supreme over the neighborhood. Appearing to be hostile and gruff, he was really putty in our hands, gentle and loving.

One day I jokingly pointed out to my husband that what Jasper needed was a little kitten to play with (preferably black, because Kris and I loved black cats—they're so sleek and shiny and special!). And guess what? I had just found one in a "free kitten" ad. Larry, who was not a cat lover, shook his head. "Jasper will never accept another cat," he said. "I think you're just asking for trouble." But he didn't object, so Kris and I answered the ad and went to pick him up.

The kitten was hiding in a corner of the garage in a laundry basket. He was solid black, with a tiny nick on his chin. Kris loved him instantly. We took him home and named him "Yoda," for an outer-space character in the *Star Wars* movie series.

In the first several days, Yoda settled into our family with no effort at all. He was an adventurous kitten who liked to ride in our car with us and loved to ride in the basket of Kris's bicycle.

But Jasper did not take kindly to the newcomer. He seemed insulted to have his domain threatened and was prone to ignore Yoda, only looking up to hiss as Yoda slid into feeding time like a baseball player stealing second. Undaunted, Yoda treated Jasper like his dearly-loved older brother, always running expectantly toward him and trying to play with him. Yoda's day was complete when he could snuggle up beside Jasper on the crocheted afghan, kneading it with his paws and purring himself to sleep. Never mind that Jasper, ever superior, totally ignored him.

It was about this time that Kris, who was always quick to express herself through art, started drawing cartoons about the two cats. Kris believed that when we weren't watching them, Jasper played with Yoda, giving him advice, taking pleasure in his company. And so Kris's drawings showed a kindly, older cat telling the "new cat on the block" important things about life, things like God's love and the need to pray and sing praises. There were cartoons of Jasper wearing a cape and flying through the sky on secret missions, with Yoda on his back, showing him the wonders of God's creation. From that time on we dubbed him "Bat Cat."

In the second week or so, I began to think that maybe Kris had the right idea: I'd see Jasper watching Yoda intently, his ears pitched forward. Occasionally I even saw him batting Yoda playfully with his paws, and once I caught him bathing Yoda's face—but never when Jasper thought I was watching.

This was the state of affairs when, about six weeks later, Yoda, not wearing his identifying collar, wandered away, probably chasing a butterfly. Kris and I were heartbroken.

And so the search began. With each fruitless day that passed, we continued to hope and make plans for the next day. "Tomorrow we'll try this . . . or that," we said. But soon we had looked everywhere with no sign of the lost kitten. I put my arm around Kris as she buried her face in my shoulder, not wanting me to see her tears. "Mom, if I could just know that someone was taking care of him," she said. "Or if he had to die, at least know that he didn't suffer. I could even accept it if he found a good home, with someone who loved cats the way we do. But I just keep picturing him out there—all alone—and it hurts so bad."

I knew exactly how she felt and realized then that I was worried not only about Yoda, but about Kris as well. *I need help, Lord,* I prayed silently. *Just give me wisdom. I can't do this anymore, so I'm giving it all to you. Please help me trust you and find words now that will help Kris.*

Turning to her, I began, "Kris, we must give this problem to Jesus. He cares, and he really is the only one who knows the whole situation. Can you believe—even if you never see Yoda again—that he just went for a walk with Jesus? Can you trust that Jesus will take care of him?"

We prayed together then. Just a simple prayer, asking Jesus to take care of Yoda. And I hugged Kris.

I really didn't expect what happened next. Kris's face lit up for the first time in days and she raced from the room. Cartoons began flying off her notebook paper again, as she grasped the concept of a little black cat "going for a walk with Jesus."

There were pictures of Jesus and Yoda—riding a bike together, frolicking through heaven (to the dismay of several angels), taking a nap on the clouds, and sitting at the table eating together.

So clearly did these drawings reflect her happiness—and

faith—that as she shared them with me, we began to laugh, and then cry at the same time. It was with complete trust that Kris said, "Mom, it's okay. I know that if I never see Yoda again, Jesus will take care of him."

Yes, I thought, *it is okay*. Only God could have chosen such a unique way of answering my prayer. What a beautiful reminder that, no matter what my own problems, God will always have a custom-designed, just-for-me answer.

Then, ten days after Yoda disappeared, a telephone call came from Mary Sims, a cat-loving woman who had just read our ad in the weekly paper. We rushed over to find Yoda happily playing on the patio with her cats on what looked like a feline gymnasium.

Together we learned that, to get to her house, Yoda had crossed three very busy main streets, had traveled one and a half miles (in a direction we hadn't even looked), and had narrowly missed being hit by several cars, as his rescuer watched helplessly from her kitchen window.

Many times Mary had attempted to coax him from his hiding place with food, but, having been chased into thick ivy by dogs, Yoda was terrified. Finally she was able to rescue the starving kitten and take him home with her.

A peek into our home that evening, after we brought Yoda back, would have revealed quite a scene. As Yoda was put down on the floor, a look of wonderment crossed his face. He looked around and sniffed the air for a few minutes. Suddenly he ran toward the kitchen and slid into the feeding dish like a baseball player stealing second. Yes, Jasper was there, but this time he licked Yoda's face as if to say, "Welcome home."

Later, we put the two cats in the garage, where they always slept at night in baskets on top of the chest freezer. Next morning, on his way to the car, Larry let the cats into the house. As Kris and I bent to kiss them, we were met with the lingering odor of after-shave lotion wafting from their foreheads. . . . We just looked at each other and smiled.

Easter Cat

Janet Streed

O f all the wild cats that had roamed our farm in the shadows of the Rockies, one in particular stole our hearts. The little calico cat meowed at us while we did chores. When our twelve-year-old daughter, Kristi, scratched her ears one morning, the kitty purred ardently. "Her name will be Pancake," Kristi announced, remembering what she'd just had for breakfast.

The friendly cat often followed Kristi around during that long Colorado winter. When at last the earth burst forth with new life, it seemed only right that Pancake gave new life too—a lively litter of healthy kittens. We put them in a box in a warm corner of the basement near the furnace. I'd never seen Kristi so excited. She knelt beside the box watching Pancake nurse the tiny, wriggling creatures.

One day during Holy Week, Kristi came running. "Mommy, something's the matter with Pancake." Sure enough, Pancake was stretched out on the floor beside the box, her kittens wailing.

I took Pancake to the vet. "She's got internal damage, probably from an injury before she came to live with you," the vet said. "Having kittens just made it worse."

Kristi and I used an eyedropper to feed the kittens. "Your mama will be home from the vet soon, kitties," Kristi promised them. "God will make her all better."

The vet wasn't so sure. "I've done what I can, but Pancake's still a very sick cat. Be prepared for the worst."

Kristi helped me get Pancake settled into a cardboard box on the far side of the basement away from the kittens. It took all her energy to lick Kristi's finger. "You'll be okay tomorrow," Kristi said, stroking Pancake's bony form. "It's Easter."

I grew up on a farm. I'd been around animals enough to know when death was near. *Poor little Pancake, Lord, and poor Kristi. Nothing she's ever loved has died.*

"Honey," I said that afternoon as we colored Easter eggs, "Pancake is very sick. The vet says she might die."

"Pancake will be okay," Kristi repeated. "It's Easter." I looked down at the egg I was dyeing. How many times had I told Kristi that Easter was about new life? Of course she was sure Pancake would live.

I went to the basement one last time before bed. The kittens were sleeping in a silky heap. Pancake lay motionless in her box. I put my hand on her, longing to feel her purr like she did that first morning. Her breathing was barely a tremor.

Just before dawn I slipped out of bed and went to the basement. I didn't want Kristi to find Pancake, not on Easter morning. But her box was empty! Had she found the strength to drag herself into a corner to die? Upstairs, I heard the others getting up. I'd break the news to them, then search for Pancake's lifeless body.

I checked on the kittens. I probably looked nearly as surprised as the women who went to Jesus' tomb that first Easter morning. "Meow." Looking up at me with bright, round eyes was a purring Pancake! Nursing contentedly were her kittens.

I raced up the stairs two at a time, crying, "Kristi, come see Pancake!"

It's Easter, I thought. *Come see the miracle of new life.* Then again, my daughter already knew all about that—better than I did.

The Calico Cure

Kathryn T. Smith

My mother was a happy woman who never seemed to mind growing old. "But my forty-eighth year was traumatic," she often joked with an exaggerated frown. "I became a grandmother." She didn't let arthritis stop her from planning family picnics and trips of all kinds. She loved fishing, gardening, and bird watching—anything to do with the outdoors.

Eventually Mother had to slow down, but she never lost her good humor. In 1985, when she was in her early seventies, doctors advised a knee-joint replacement. After much thought and prayer, Mother decided to go ahead with the surgery.

While she was in the hospital, she contracted a staph infection in the new joint. With physical therapy her walking improved, but nothing would heal the infection. Mother became withdrawn and depressed. Our whole family prayed for a way to help her.

One day she was sitting alone in the backyard, wondering if she'd ever feel like herself again. "Suddenly," she told us later, "this cat was just there in the middle of the yard." It was a beautiful, long-haired calico. *Must be the neighbor's,* Mother assumed. But when she called, the neighbor said her cat was asleep on the sofa. Mother tried shooing the animal away. The cat wouldn't budge.

When she couldn't find the owner, Mother decided to make friends. "Calico," she coaxed, but the cat was shy. Finally, after being bribed with a can of tuna, the cat ventured almost within Mother's reach.

Every day after that, Calico showed up to be fed, and soon let Mother pet her. When the cat saw Mother come out the back door, she would run to Mother's chair. Calico would wait for her to sit down and then she'd roll over on her back and purr, begging to have her tummy scratched.

"Why does that cat get more attention than I do?" Daddy kidded. "She never complains, that's why," Mother retorted.

Calico didn't befriend anyone else in the family. She allowed no one but Mother to touch her, which Mother found quite amusing.

Not long after Calico arrived on the scene, Mother went into the hospital for two weeks for another knee surgery to replace the infected joint, and then to a care center for two weeks more. While she was gone, Calico appeared every morning on the back step. Daddy put food out for her, but the cat wouldn't come near him. When Mother returned home in a wheelchair, Calico endured the indignity of being picked up by one of us and placed in Mother's lap. The cat had never sat in her lap before, but now she purred contentedly, as if that were where she belonged.

Calico was my mother's constant companion during

that long year of recovery. "My angel of mercy," Mother called her. One day, after the doctors had pronounced her fully recovered, Mother decided the cat should have a checkup, too, and made an appointment at the vet. The next morning, however, Calico was nowhere to be found. We never saw her again, but I often think of her—an answer to our prayers.

The Box

Mary Louise Kitsen

There's more to do than I can handle," I said, loudly and clearly. Of course, there was no one to hear my complaint except the three cats lying on the bed. Two of them continued sleeping while the third laid her ears back and switched her tail.

I sighed. There were writing assignments to be done (I'm a full-time freelance writer), my cousins were coming from Kansas in a few days, and I had to clean the entire house. And my mother was in the hospital again, which meant two trips there each day. How would I get to everything?

Deciding that Jesus was the only one who could help, I addressed him directly. "With your help, I'll make it, but please don't let anything else happen right now."

It was still early in the morning. I slipped my robe on and started downstairs. Maybe if I relaxed briefly with some toast and coffee, taking a look at the morning paper at the same time, I'd feel ready to tackle the busy day ahead. I opened the door and picked up the newspaper. Then I saw the box.

Where did it come from? It was a large box with "Corn Flakes" written on the side. An old, rusted window screen lay on top; a rope kept it in place. *Oh, no . . . someone who knows how I feel about cats must have dumped kittens on me again. Just what I needed!*

I started to pick the box up, and when I felt how heavy it was, I realized they had dumped the mother cat too. Actually, I didn't know the half of it!

I set the box down in the living room, untied the rope, and looked in. There was a big, yellow cat. But where were her kittens? I reached in and lifted out the cat. It started to purr immediately and pushed its head tightly against my shoulder. One big cat? A male at that.

I held the cat up to take a better look at him, and I started to sob. This big, beautiful cat had no eyes—just white skin where his eyes should have been. I cradled him as my other cats started to gather. Pip-Squeak rubbed against the newcomer with evident pleasure. But what was I going to do with a blind kitty? How much care would he need?

I looked in the box to see if there was anything else and found a note: *This is Poppy. My dad hates having him around and said he'd shoot him if Mom and I didn't get rid of him ourselves. Please take care of him.* It was the handwriting of a youngster. Poor, sad child trying to keep a blind cat alive.

Poppy ate with the other cats—to my surprise and relief—and I showed him the litter box. I got absolutely nothing done before it was time to leave for the hospital, and I worried about leaving the cat in a strange place. But he seemed content and interested in investigating things. I called the vet's office and made an appointment. Then I left, praying that Poppy would make out all right.

When I returned home, I found Poppy sleeping with Pip-Squeak in the sunny dining room window. In the early afternoon I put him in a carrier and headed for the vet's office. I hated to take him, but I had to have help in this matter. The vet took him into a back room to check him over. I sat straight as a pin, not knowing what to expect.

The vet finally came out. He was alone. My heart did a flip-flop. *What about Poppy?* At that moment I realized the big yellow cat had stolen my heart.

"Someone took good care of that fellow," the doctor told me. "He's in good shape and amazingly contented. We'll keep him a couple days. He should be altered and have some shots, and there are a few tests we'd like to do."

I grinned.

Then the bomb fell. "We think Poppy is deaf and dumb as well as blind."

For the next two days I wondered how I'd manage a pet that couldn't see, hear, or make a sound. I prayed about the cat. And, to my surprise, I was getting an awful lot of things accomplished even though my mind stayed on Poppy. It was as if Poppy were a challenge, and so everything else was a challenge too.

I brought Poppy and my mother home from their respective hospitals just two days later. I went for Mom first and got her settled in her favorite chair in the living room. Then I went for Poppy.

Mom moved to the edge of her chair as I brought the carrier in. I opened it and Poppy climbed into my arms. How he loved people! I carried him over to Mom and she gathered him to her. In minutes, Poppy purred happily on her lap. It was the start of a warm, personal friendship between an elderly lady and a handicapped kitty-cat—a relationship that has made both of their lives happier.

Poppy had helped me too. I was feeling sorry for myself when he came, but through him I gained a better attitude. It seemed almost as if Jesus had guided Poppy's owners to bring him to me. Little by little, I began to think more and more about the mother and child who had left Poppy in my care. Who were they? Would they wonder about what had happened to Poppy?

Then one day I made a sign that read, *Poppy is fine*, and I taped it to my front porch. I hoped the youngster who had brought the cat to me would see it.

The sign stayed up for several days. Then came the morning I went outside to the garage and saw something that made my life even better. Written on the bottom of the sign I'd made were two messages, evidently written by the child and his mother—at least, that's what I've always thought. The child's writing said, *Thank you*. The adult's hand wrote, *God Bless You*.

Bill's Christmas Miracle

Bill Edwards

In the basement of my apartment building in New York City, I discovered a colony of wild cats. Moved by their plight, I began feeding them; but conditions down there became so that the cats were all infested with fleas and getting sick. One by one I trapped them, took them to the vet, and had them cleaned up, inoculated, and neutered.

One of them, a female kitten I named Cleopatra, I brought home to my family, but she was so feral that I had to keep her locked in the bathroom so she wouldn't attack my other cats. I tried to get close to her, to stroke her, and to show her that she wasn't in any danger, that she had found a home and that she was loved. But she didn't trust anybody. Cleo wouldn't let me even touch her; she clawed me and bit me whenever I got too close. My hands and arms were covered in scratches and teeth marks.

Finally, when she had calmed down somewhat, I thought it was time to let Cleo have access to the rest of the apartment. The moment she was out of the bathroom she dashed under my bed and wouldn't leave, hiding there, refusing to come out even to eat. I wound up putting a food

114

bowl and a litter pan under the bed, but that was an unsatis-
factory arrangement.

What I really wanted was to have Cleo join the family
and be my pet, but I saw that I'd have to start from scratch
(and I mean scratch!). Figuring she'd have to go back to
confinement in the bathroom for a while, I set up a small cat
carrier there and pushed her food dish farther and farther
back into it with each meal.

On Christmas Eve 1995, I decided to attend the Blessing
of the Animals at Central Presbyterian Church—and to bring
her along with me. Maybe in the presence of all those contented
animals and devoted animal lovers Cleo would feel safe and
begin to calm down and not be so frightened. I have always
believed there is something divine in the communion between
people and animals—maybe this would bring it out in Cleo.

That evening, before going to the blessing, I sat and
meditated, focusing entirely on the hope that Cleopatra
would heal and be unafraid, that she would someday allow me
to touch her.

With Cleo in the carrier, I took the subway from
Brooklyn to Manhattan to the Central Presbyterian Church
on Park Avenue and Sixty-fourth Street. On the train I took
off my glove, baring my hand laced with scars and scratches,
and tentatively opened Cleo's box. Slowly, I put my bare hand
in and touched her very lightly on the back, and—

Nothing. No hissing, no biting, none of her usual wild
and frantic scratching. No distrust at all. Just an amazing
peace and quiet and the feel of her warm fur under my fingers.

My heart leaped as I realized that for the first time Cleopatra was allowing me to pet her. All during the train ride, I stroked her quietly. Once we were in the church, the woman sitting next to me put her hand into the carrier and stroked Cleo. Cleo accepted the stroking quietly and without resistance. On the train ride home from the blessing it occurred to me that I had a new cat. A shy, scared cat, but my cat.

That night, I was asleep in bed when I woke up to a weight pressing against me. It was Cleo, curled up against my body and purring like a small engine as Christmas morning came. A great feeling of relief and gratitude washed over me as I received this little creature's love. From that night on, it was as though she'd always been with me and had never once been wild. All her fears were forgotten. Cleo was a sweet, gentle, loving pussycat. She was home.

To this day, I believe Cleo was a gift from God. My Christmas miracle.

Lessons Learned

from Cats

A Lesson in Love

Pam Johnson

Mr. Vinsley was one of the most memorable clients I've ever known. Originally from England, he was an older man who had been a widower for many years and lived in a beautiful mansion in Kentucky.

"My problem is very unusual," he said at the beginning of our phone call, but he refused to go into any greater detail.

"Please, Mr. Vinsley," I urged him, "I prefer to have an idea of what behavior a cat is displaying in case I feel a visit to the vet is needed."

"I promise you, a vet is not required for this situation," he replied. Pausing a moment, he added, "I assure you, I'm not a crackpot."

I began to discuss my fee with him, but he interrupted again. "It doesn't matter—I'll pay whatever you charge."

I explained to him that if I got to his house and I felt a vet visit was required, I'd have to reschedule our session. He agreed. Four days later I was headed to Kentucky.

The Vinsley residence was located on a beautiful and secluded road. The long driveway led up to a magnificent house. There were two cars parked in the driveway—

a shining, black Mercedes and a dusty, gray Honda. I parked next to the Honda.

I was greeted at the door by the housekeeper. She eyed my armful of cat toys and raised an eyebrow.

"I'm the feline behavior consultant," I said with a smile.

"The cat shrink," she corrected me.

I was led into the living room, where I was told Mr. Vinsley would join me shortly. I sat down on the huge couch and glanced around the antique-filled room. Massive pieces of furniture dominated the long walls. Each vase and statue looked as if it held a fascinating history. Heavy draperies hung from the large windows, blocking the sun. I felt as if I were in a museum.

While I waited for Mr. Vinsley to appear, I neatly arranged all my cat toys on the carpet next to the couch. My notebook was opened, and my pen sat ready to take down client history. All I needed was my client. So I waited. And waited. My client was now twelve minutes late.

The housekeeper reappeared in the doorway. "Mr. Vinsley apologizes for the delay. He'll be with you directly," she said coolly. "Would you care for something to drink?"

"No, thank you," I replied, and the housekeeper disappeared quickly.

Another ten minutes went by. I found myself starting to get sleepy. The sofa was quite comfortable and the room rather dark. "I'll give him five more minutes and then I'm leaving," I said to myself, or at least I thought I'd said it to myself.

"Forgive me, Miss Johnson."

I jerked my head up and looked in the direction of the voice with the British accent. In the doorway stood a very distinguished, thin man in a three-piece suit. I guessed his age to be late seventies. He had a full head of silver hair, combed very stylishly. He stepped toward me, offering his hand. "Please forgive my rudeness," he said as we greeted each other. "I had to take a very important but rather annoying phone call."

"I understand." I nodded. "Now, why don't we get started?" I began to reach for my notebook, but he stood up and started for the door.

"Let's have some tea," he said. "Or would you prefer coffee?"

I started to say that I had already declined his housekeeper's offer, but he wouldn't take no for an answer. So tea it was.

As we drank our tea and ate cookies baked by the housekeeper (who shot me another skeptical look when she brought in the tray), I began to question Mr. Vinsley about his cat. "What behavior has your cat been displaying?" I asked, preparing to take notes.

"Oh, he's a fine cat," he stated as he took a bite of cookie. "There's nothing wrong with his behavior."

I looked up from my notebook. "There's nothing wrong with his behavior?"

He saw my reaction and leaned back in his chair. "I do have a problem with my cat, but it doesn't have anything to do with his behavior."

"All right, then. How can I help you?" I was tempted to remind him that I was, after all, a feline behavior consultant, but there was something about this man I liked. He seemed sincere. Sincere about what, I didn't know, but sincere nonetheless.

"I need you to find a good home for my cat."

I took off my glasses and rubbed my eyes. "Mr. Vinsley, I don't handle animal adoptions. I deal with animal behavior. I can give you the names of some wonderful people I know who—"

"No," he interrupted. "I specifically want you to find him a home."

"Why me?"

"Miss Johnson, I've read your books, seen you on TV, and heard about the work you do. You really understand cats. My cat, Dancer, is all I have, and I want the very best for him. I'll pay you for all the time you spend searching."

I was confused. "Why do you need to find him another home?"

Mr. Vinsley looked at me. I saw his eyes get misty for just a moment, and then he regained his composure. "Mr. Vinsley, are you all right?" I asked.

"I have cancer," he said in almost a whisper. He then went on to explain his reason for calling me. His doctor had told him he had less than nine months to live. He was not afraid to die, he assured me. After all, he had lived a good seventy-seven years. He had every comfort, had never wanted for anything, and was willing to face the end of his life with dignity. All of his business was in order. He had no family and wanted the money from his estate to go to cancer research, children's charities, and several animal-welfare organizations.

"There's just one important thing left to do," Mr. Vinsley said sadly. "I need to take care of Dancer. I found him four years ago and we've been best friends ever since. I need you to find him a home while I'm still alive. I want to know for sure that he'll be getting the love and care he deserves. I'll provide for his medical and food expenses." He looked down at his hands and then at me. "I know anyone else would think I'm a foolish old man, worrying about some cat, but he's been by my side through these very tough last years. When I was too sick to get out of bed, Dancer stayed right with me. He's a wonderful friend, and I want to make sure he lives a good life without me."

I didn't know what to say. Mr. Vinsley stood up, breaking my awkward silence.

"I'll introduce you to Dancer." With that, he left the room.

It was then I realized I'd been holding my breath as he'd been talking. I hadn't been expecting anything like this.

A few minutes later Mr. Vinsley came back, holding a gray cat in his arms. Dancer was a tough-looking male cat who had obviously seen more than his share of fights before becoming a resident at the Vinsley home. He was a huge cat, not fat, but tall and large. Both ears were torn at the tips and his nose bore several old scars.

Despite his rough exterior, Dancer's personality was sweet and gentle. Wrapped in his owner's arms, his loud purr sounded like an old car engine. Mr. Vinsley placed him on the floor, and the cat walked right over to greet me. Not content with just being petted, Dancer jumped into my lap and nuzzled me with his face.

Mr. Vinsley had found Dancer sitting on his car one cold winter morning. Having no fondness for cats at all, he promptly chased Dancer off the car, and that was that. Or so Mr. Vinsley thought. Every morning for the next week, there was this gray cat sitting on the roof of his beautiful Mercedes.

One morning as Mr. Vinsley watched the news on TV from his bed, he heard that the temperature would continue to drop during the day. It would be frigid by evening. Even though he didn't like cats, he hated the thought that the poor creature might freeze outside. Surely he must belong to someone. Mr. Vinsley planned on telling the owner of the cat to keep him on his own property. Perhaps he has a collar, Mr. Vinsley thought. So he quickly dressed and went out, fully expecting to find the big gray cat lounging on his car as usual. He opened the front door, felt the blast of cold air, and looked out. No cat.

Mr. Vinsley had never liked animals, and yet he found himself checking outside every few minutes, waiting for the cat. He kept telling himself that all he wanted to do was to find the owner of this pesky feline.

When the housekeeper arrived home from her morning shopping, she found Mr. Vinsley in the kitchen in his robe, spooning tuna into a dish. She didn't ask him what he was doing. He hadn't been eating well lately, so if he wanted to eat tuna at seven in the morning, why bother him?

Mr. Vinsley hurried outside and placed the dish of tuna on the roof of his car, then went back to his warm house to wait. His plan was to take the cat to the local shelter if it had no identification. He'd be rid of that stray one way or the other.

A widower for twenty-five years, Mr. Vinsley had also outlived his only son. With no grandchildren and no surviving relatives, he was very used to a life of solitude. He spent his days reading, listening to music, and walking around the beautiful grounds surrounding his house. He was comfortable being alone and was not at all interested in making friends or engaging in silly chatter with neighbors. His housekeeper jokingly referred to him as "Scrooge."

By the end of the day, the tuna, now quite frozen, was removed from the car. The housekeeper watched but knew better than to say anything.

"Have it your way, you stupid cat," Mr. Vinsley said as he went back inside the house and dumped the can in the garbage. Just before going to bed that night, he stuck his head out the front door one more time to check for the annoying cat. He wasn't out there, so Mr. Vinsley locked the door and went to bed.

At about 2:00 A.M., Mr. Vinsley woke up. He swears it was a terrible thirst that drove him out of bed and down the stairs to the kitchen. Along the way, he stopped for a quick peek out the front door—still no cat sitting on the car. But just as Mr. Vinsley was about to close the door, he caught sight of something limping toward him. Hobbling up the driveway was the gray cat. His fur was matted and his right front paw dangled helplessly in the air. Mr. Vinsley stepped out onto the porch, but as soon as he did, the gray cat stopped.

"I'm not going to hurt you," he said to the cat. "Come here and I'll help you."

The cat just looked at him, not moving. Mr. Vinsley didn't know if he should go in to get more food. What if the cat ran off? But he knew he had to do something soon—the cold air was going right through his thin robe.

Leaving the front door open, he slowly stepped into the house and padded into the kitchen, where he dumped some leftover chicken onto a large plate. He was afraid the cat would be gone, but when he got back to the front porch, there the cat was, standing in the driveway with his paw in the air.

Mr. Vinsley placed the food on the porch and leaned against the doorway. The old man and the cat just looked at each other.

Mr. Vinsley really hadn't cared about anybody in a long time, and he didn't know why he was so concerned about this cat now. There was just something about him. Yet here were these two tough old guys, so used to being alone that they didn't even know how to ask for help.

"I generally don't care for your kind, you know," Mr. Vinsley said to the hesitant feline. "But, please, let me help you. Come on, it's too cold for me to be out here."

A few minutes passed. Mr. Vinsley was shivering. The cat was watching him intently; he seemed to be making a decision.

The old gray cat limped up to the porch, sniffed at the plate of food, then weakly hobbled past it and through the open doorway.

Amazed that the cat had voluntarily walked into the house, Mr. Vinsley followed him in and closed the door. "I don't blame you for passing up the chicken," he said to the cat. "Regina's not a very good cook."

After some hesitation, the cat allowed Mr. Vinsley to examine his injured paw. It would need medical attention first thing in the morning. In the meantime, the scruffy old thing would spend the night in the kitchen. As Mr. Vinsley bent down to scoop him up, he darted off on his three good legs in the direction of the stairs. Before he could be stopped, he clumsily hobbled up toward the bedrooms.

Planning to retrieve the nuisance cat in a moment, Mr. Vinsley went back to lock the front door. Cold and tired, he then climbed the stairs. Figuring that the frightened cat would be hiding under the beds, he switched on the light to begin his search. But the cat had already decided that being on the bed was much more comfortable. There he was, curled up at the foot of the huge bed.

"You could've at least chosen one of the guest rooms," Mr. Vinsley commented. But he was too tired to argue, so he crawled under the covers, stretched his feet out next to the cat, and turned out the light. "Don't get too used to this. You're leaving in the morning."

The following morning, on the way to his own doctor's appointment, Mr. Vinsley dropped the cat off at the nearest veterinary hospital.

It was at this visit to the doctor that Mr. Vinsley learned he had cancer. Depressed and frightened, he drove home, almost forgetting to stop at the vet's. In fact, when he realized he was about to pass the animal hospital, he seriously considered just leaving the cat there for the vet to deal with. But he stopped anyway.

The gray cat had a broken leg. When the veterinary technician brought him out he was sporting a large splint. Mr. Vinsley paid the bill and left with the cat. Even though he didn't understand why, he felt a tug at his heart when he held the cat in his arms.

Three weeks into the new relationship, Mr. Vinsley's health took a serious turn for the worse and he was confined to his bed. The cat, by now named "Dancer"—because he could move so gracefully despite his heavy splint—left Mr. Vinsley's side only to use his litter box and grab a generous amount of food. The friendship grew deeper and deeper. When Mr. Vinsley was well enough, the pair would stroll around the grounds or sit in the sun. Dancer loved to sleep in Mr. Vinsley's lap when he listened to classical music or read a book.

And another thing happened. Mr. Vinsley started chatting with neighbors about pets. They'd share stories and advice. After all these years, Mr. Vinsley was caring about others again. Soon his neighbors became friends who would often stop by for a cup of coffee or to play cards.

As I listened to Mr. Vinsley talk about Dancer, I promised myself I'd do everything I could to fulfill his wish.

I made several trips to visit Mr. Vinsley and Dancer. We'd have tea together and talk. I loved those afternoon visits and think of them often.

After a lengthy search, I found a potential home for Dancer—a sweet and gentle woman who had lost her husband years earlier. I thought it was a wonderful chance for Dancer to give this lonely person the same gift of love he'd given to Mr. Vinsley.

When Ruth Leeson met Mr. Vinsley and Dancer, all three of them hit it off. They spent much time together, and Mr. Vinsley took great pleasure in telling Ruth all about Dancer's likes and dislikes.

Eight months after I first met Mr. Vinsley, he was taken to the hospital. His housekeeper phoned to tell me that Mr. Vinsley wanted me to come get Dancer and take him to his new home. I canceled my appointments for the day, then called Ruth to tell her to expect Dancer.

I drove to the Vinsley residence. The housekeeper let me in and I collected Dancer's things. As if he knew what was about to happen, Dancer was waiting for me in Mr. Vinsley's room. He sat quietly on the bed. The housekeeper walked me to my car. She touched my arm and thanked me for helping Mr. Vinsley. There were tears in her eyes. She'd worked for him for fifteen years.

Later that day I visited Mr. Vinsley in the hospital to tell him that Dancer was in his new home and that Ruth was doing everything she could to make him feel at home. He smiled. We talked a little while longer and then he drifted off to sleep. I quietly got up and stood by the bed for a few moments. "I'll keep watch over Dancer for you," I whispered, and left him to rest.

Two days later Mr. Vinsley died.

I've since visited Dancer in his new home several times, and he's very happy. He follows Ruth the same way he did Mr. Vinsley. And I've noticed that Ruth looks much more content than when I first met her. She proudly told me that Dancer sleeps on his own pillow next to her in bed.

Dancer, the once scruffy, tough stray cat, taught Mr. Vinsley how to love again. And now, the furry gray teacher with torn ears and a purr like an old car engine is helping Ruth to learn that same lesson.

Leo the Lionhearted

Susan DeVore Williams

First, you should know that this isn't just another cat story. The main character is, I admit, my Siamese cat, Leo. I can't tell you that Leo ever dragged me from a burning building or croaked his deafening Siamese meow to warn me of an impending earthquake. But God has used him to teach me a lesson it's taken me twenty years to learn, and not many cats can be that kind of hero.

From the moment our eyes met through the pet shop window in Minneapolis on a cold spring day in 1964, I knew this sealpoint kitten was something special. He struggled and protested loudly as the shopkeeper pulled him from his cage.

"He may be small," I laughed, "but he seems to have the heart of a lion."

"He has the voice of a lion too," the shopkeeper said. And so I named him Leo the Lionhearted. Even his birthday seemed symbolic: Valentine's Day.

My husband and I were childless and, as often happens, we became more than casually attached to Leo. He managed to fit himself into every area of our lives effortlessly and completely. I grew to expect his noisy greeting at the door each evening and enjoyed his flattering, rapt attention when I wandered around our apartment doing housework. He even developed an awareness of my moods, pawing at my leg to be picked up when he sensed I needed comforting, then patting my cheek with his paw.

Sometimes I'd catch myself carrying on an animated conversation with Leo as he perched on a chair and gazed at me. "If I could be that kind of listener," I told him, "I'd be the most popular woman in town." And Leo never disagreed with me.

In his third year, Leo stayed with my parents while we were away on an extended business trip. When we picked him up he was listless and very thin. My father had tried everything to coax him to eat, to no avail. His belly seemed bloated, and within a few hours it had grown so large he had trouble sitting down. I called his veterinarian. "Bring him to my office now," he said.

At the clinic, the vet made a quick diagnosis: a kidney stone. "Another hour and he'll be dead unless I take some emergency measures. I don't guarantee anything. He's in a lot of pain. Do you want me to go ahead and catheterize him, or should I put him to sleep?"

I stood in numbed silence. Words wouldn't come. Finally, I shook my head. "Do what you can to save him. Please."

I sat in the waiting room until, at long last, the vet returned. "I don't know what to tell you. I've catheterized him, but he's passed another stone, and I'm afraid this is going to be a chronic problem. He needs surgery, and I doubt he'll survive it. He's very underweight and weak. If it were my cat, I'd put him to sleep."

"Does he have any chance at all for recovery?" I asked.

"I'd say no," the vet said. "I'm sorry, but I know you want the truth. He may have a five or ten percent chance of surviving surgery, but he will always have this problem."

"I need some time alone with him, please," I managed to say.

When the vet left me in the examining room, I stroked Leo's fragile body and watched him breathe. Until that moment I hadn't realized how much I'd come to love my lion-hearted cat.

"Lord, I can't put him to sleep unless you tell me to," I said aloud. "You're going to have to give me some sort of confirmation, or else you're going to have to do it yourself. Show me, Lord." I waited.

Perhaps five minutes passed, and I stood stroking Leo's head. He was very still. Suddenly, a thought entered my mind: *Pray for him. Pray for his healing.* I laughed bitterly. "Pray for an animal? I'm really cracking up!"

After a few moments, my heart racing, I put both hands on Leo's body. "In the name of Jesus, you are whole. In life or in death, you belong to God. I commit your spirit to God, who created you." I paused. "Father, I ask you for Leo's life. Please restore him to health. Thank you, Lord. I trust you with his life."

The vet walked into the room as if on cue, looking expectantly at me.

"I want you to operate," I told him. "Do whatever you can to get him through the night. I'll talk with you in the morning."

"Okay," he said reluctantly. "But I don't think he'll survive the surgery."

By morning, as I prayed, my faith was about half the size of a mustard seed. I dreaded calling the vet.

"Well, sometimes animals will surprise you," he said. "He made it through the night. But he's a very, very, sick cat. I can't give you any real hope. Do you want to see him?"

Leo was an even more pitiful sight than he'd been the night before. *I should have had him put to sleep.* Deep within, I could feel God's gentle reproof: *Where is your faith? You asked me for restoration. Trust me!*

I stroked Leo's head and he slowly raised his eyes to my face.

Oh, Lord, I thought, *he trusts me so completely. Even in his pain, he trusts me. I want to be like that with you. Help me to trust you in my pain. Make me like that, Lord!*

I moved my hand under Leo's throat and ever so faintly I felt a vibration. He was purring.

The following morning, the vet called to warn me that Leo was now only four pounds, would not eat at all, and would have to be force-fed if he was to survive even another day. "It might give him an extra will to live if you took him home," he said. "Being in familiar surroundings might help."

Hastily, I prepared for Leo's return: padded box with a heating pad, bottles of baby food, eyedroppers for liquids.

"Okay, Lord," I said on the drive to pick him up. "It's up to you."

Through the next twenty-four hours I attempted to feed Leo every fifteen minutes. Because he was unable even to lick water, I squirted it into the side of his mouth. Most of it dribbled out onto the towel I'd wrapped around him. He gazed at me with unblinking eyes. I scraped baby food onto his lower teeth, but it simply lay on his gums. Finally, I sat beside Leo, unmoving, weariness sapping my strength, and I said, "Lord, should I stop? Show me. I need to know your desire, your intentions."

I put one more fingerful of food to Leo's mouth and started to open his lips. Then I watched his tongue slowly reach out and lick the food from his teeth, and then from my finger. I let out a whoop and jumped to my feet.

I had an impulse to read a Psalm of thanksgiving, and I reached for my Bible. Leafing randomly through Psalms, I began to read aloud from Psalm 50, not really thinking deeply about the words, until they began to sink in as I reached verse 10: "For every beast of the forest is mine, and the cattle upon a thousand hills or upon the mountains where thousands are. I know and am acquainted with all the birds of the mountains, and the wild animals of the field are mine and are with me, in my mind."

Stunned, I read the words again and again, feeling the heaviness lift from my heart. "Lord, how wonderful you are," I prayed. "Leo is yours, and he is always in your mind. Thank you for lending him to me, for making him my trusting friend. Thank you for showing me that I need to be that kind of trusting friend to you."

Within forty-eight hours, Leo was walking shakily and eating normally. In a week, he was recovering. In three months, his weight was up to nine pounds.

"Just don't expect this to be permanent," the vet told me when I took Leo for a checkup. "At any moment, he could get another kidney stone, and that'll be it."

Over the next two years I rejoiced in Leo's good health. But I also developed a kind of chronic fear as a result of the vet's dismal prognosis. I watched Leo daily for signs of recurrence. If he sneezed, I called the vet. Finally, toward the middle of his fifth year, it happened: the same symptoms, but I caught them before the bloating got out of hand. In a state of panic, I raced to the vet.

By this time, fear had a good grip on me. "Lord," I said, "is this it? Two short years? I thought you'd healed him completely." I felt a pang of guilt. *I'm not doing a very good job of trusting God*, I thought. *No*, I could feel the Lord saying deep inside, *you aren't*.

It turned out that Leo had a serious infection, and he nearly died again.

Leo recovered, of course. And in his seventh and ninth and twelfth years, he had similar brushes with death. Each time, my confidence in God's intentions grew. But the fear didn't leave entirely. I prayed over and over that God would remove it.

In Leo's sixteenth year, we moved to California. There, my life entered a phase that hardly seemed real. My husband of eighteen years left me. But I got custody of Leo. Once again, he spent long hours at my side, comforting me with his presence.

Then, just a few weeks after my husband's departure, Leo developed symptoms of infection. "No, Lord!" I cried. "I can't go through this now! Don't take him away from me! Don't do this!" Fear seemed more powerful than ever. I was so distraught that without pausing to think, I found myself speaking in a loud, angry voice: "Stop it! Just stop."

Who—or what—was I speaking to?

Fear, I thought. *That's what.*

"Stop," I said again, angrier than ever. "Fear, I am sick of you. This cat doesn't belong to me. He belongs to God. The Lord has healed and restored him over and over again, when everyone said it was hopeless. So it's time you just got lost."

Amazed at my own words, I smiled. And then I felt it. The fear had departed. I was calm. I gathered up my lion-hearted cat and told him, "Don't worry. You're going to be fine. As usual."

But that night, as I lay in bed, the emotional pain of my broken marriage began to overwhelm me. Leo would be all right, I knew, but what about me? I was nearly forty, without any kind of support system in this strange city. I had no future, no career, no money, no home, and my friends and family were more than two thousand miles away. "Lord," I whispered into the night, "what will become of me? I'm so afraid."

Leo padded from the foot of the bed toward my face. His cold nose touched my chin. In the darkness, he settled down to comfort me again. "Leo, I'm so scared," I told him. "I'm so scared." He purred and licked my cheek. Slowly, the truth began to dawn on me.

God had taught me to trust him with my cat's life. It had taken most of Leo's proverbial nine lives to do it. Each time he'd approached the brink of death and all had seemed hopeless, God had done the impossible. I could almost hear him say, "How many times are you going to have to go through this before you finally learn to trust me?"

And God had been as present in my life as in Leo's! Events crowded through my mind as incident after incident played out like a movie. Time and again the Lord had met my need—and in ways I'd never expected. Had he ever abandoned me? Had he ever failed to provide food, clothing, shelter, work, friends, or everything else I needed? Had he ever broken his promises?

I hugged Leo close. "We're going to be okay," I whispered.

And we were.

Valentine's Day 1984 was Leo's twentieth birthday. He's had skirmishes with death in the last four years, but the fear has not returned. His new vet pronounces him one of the Seven Wonders of the World.

"He's probably your oldest friend," the vet said on her last visit to check Leo. "It's going to be terribly difficult for you when he finally goes."

I thought about that. Yes, it will be hard. It can't be

anything else. But the fear—well, we've gotten through that together, Leo and I. And we've learned about trusting God, together. The Bible told me that Leo is always in God's mind, and in a loving and miraculous way, God has revealed his mind to me through this lionhearted cat.

I scratched Leo's ears and smiled. The vet stroked him admiringly.

"I'll say this for him," she said. "He's sure lived up to his name."

The Cat Who
Wouldn't Come Out

Christine Conti

W hen my next-door neighbor Sally begged me to take in a homeless cat, I was almost ready to end our friendship.

I was tired of flea-ridden animals with sad eyes and dirty coats. I had adopted, rehabilitated, and found homes for more of them than I cared to admit. I was just getting reacquainted with my own neglected cats, and planning my return to daily prayer and Bible study, when Sally showed up. She sat on my couch staring apologetically into her coffee cup as she gave me the details.

The cat had been cherished by the Hetricks, an elderly couple who lived down the street. The wife had entered a nursing home, and now her husband was sick and needed care himself. They had no children, just some in-laws who were allergic to cats and were thinking of putting the pet in a shelter. "But people don't go to shelters looking for twelve-year-old cats," Sally said. "She'll be destroyed. I'd take her, but my cat Maggie hates other cats. Yours, though, are used to strangers."

"Well, sort of," I said. It had only taken a week for them

to emerge from under the bed when I brought the last stray home. I smiled at Sally and thought about moving.

"Her name's Ebony," she said. "She's black with a splash of white on her chest."

"Oh, all right," I said, as if this were the deciding point. "I'll take her, but just till I find her another home." Actually, it was the plight of the elderly couple that moved me: I often wondered who would care for my animals if I couldn't.

Sally and I made plans to meet the cat-allergic in-laws who were temporarily caring for the Hetricks' house and Ebony. Sally left, and I went upstairs to prepare an unused bedroom—cats need their own space. The room was empty except for some rolled-up carpets and boxes of winter clothes. Muttering under my breath about yet another burden, I arranged a jumble of boxes, plastic milk crates, and old blankets to provide a variety of hiding and sleeping places. Then I grabbed a cat carrier and was off.

When I got to the Hetricks' house, the in-laws told me Ebony had been hiding in the cellar for as long as they had been there—about two weeks. *Uh-oh*, I thought, *not a friendly cat*.

Sally and I were able to extract a cat-shaped mop of long black fur from underneath the furnace, get her into the cat carrier, and release her into my upstairs room. She immediately dashed for a milk crate behind the pile of rolled-up carpets. My cats, Damian and Mookie, were furious and alternated between rushing the pile, hissing furiously, and beating a terrified retreat to cower in my room.

Frankly, I felt about the same; a new cat meant more food, litter, and visits to the vet. What had I been thinking?

My resentment softened when I unpacked her things. She had a well-worn, often-repaired toy mouse, a carpet in the shape and colors of a rainbow, and, most heart-tugging of all, a handmade label on her food canister which read in fancy, crayoned letters: "Ebony—Our Pride and Joy!" All my previous refugees had been unwanted and uncared for; this was a cat that had been loved.

It wasn't an easy few weeks. Ebony was so unfriendly. Except for the necessities, which she accomplished at night, Ebony wouldn't leave her crate behind the carpet, much less her room. How was I going to find a home for her? What sort of ads and signs could I write? "Aging, unfriendly cat needs loving home"?

I bought toys, tried homeopathic remedies, positioned a mirror on the floor by the doorway so she could see from inside her room that the hall outside was cat-free. . . . Nothing worked. Mookie and Damian didn't help either—they got over their fear and hostility but avoided her room. My vet told me that Ebony might come out in a few months, or she just might stay in that room for the rest of her life. I prayed for inspiration, and an old saying popped to mind: if the mountain wouldn't come to me, I would go to the mountain. Perhaps if I spent some time in the room with Ebony every day, she'd get used to me and come out.

At first I didn't know what I'd do in there. There was no TV, radio, stereo, or sewing machine, not even a chair. *I'll take in a book*, I thought. *The Bible*.

I brought a lamp into the room and perched it on a box. Then I sat next to it on the floor, resting my back against the pile of rolled-up carpets. I twisted around and reached into Ebony's crate to pet her and say hello. Then I turned back and read Scripture and prayed. It was wonderfully peaceful, and I stayed much longer than I had intended.

For the next few days, right after breakfast, I had my quiet time in what I had come to think of as Ebony's room. Soon it was a firm habit. I became so absorbed in reading and praying that, one day, when Ebony crept out of hiding and sat cautiously a few feet away from me, I barely noticed. When I finished my prayers, I got my first really good look at her: a solidly built, long-haired black cat with springy whiskers and a dusting of white on her chest.

It wasn't long before Ebony jumped out of her box when I appeared, purred, rolled around happily, and curled up next to me while I prayed and read. One day I came across the admonition: "And let us not be weary in well doing: for in due season we shall reap, if we faint not" (Galatians 6:9). I looked at Ebony, whom I had so resented, who had made me feel so weary, and thanked God for sending her and restoring to me my quiet time.

That was three months ago. Ebony is now a permanent part of my home—though she isn't out of her room yet. But even if she never ventures into the rest of the house, I will continue to go to her. My visits there are the high point of my day—not just because of the time I spend with Ebony, though I've come to dote on her, but because of the time I spend with God.

Scaredy-Cat

Jeanette Doyle Parr

When my daughter Kathey brought home a kitten she'd found, we were going through a family crisis. Ill health had just forced my forty-five-year-old husband, Byzie, into retirement. From now on he would be staying home and undergoing more treatments. I was determined to keep our daily life normal and to act as if nothing was the matter.

I smiled as Kathey put the gray-and-white ball of fluff down on the den floor. "Her name is Tejas," Kathey said. "It's an old Spanish word for friendly."

Our two other cats padded over for a sniff. Bear was a half-Siamese giant who permitted our fourteen-year-old son, Alan, to be his slave, and Midnight was a black rogue who owned Kristan, our eleven-year-old daughter.

But Tejas, it soon became apparent, had not learned the meaning of her name. Her hair stiffened like porcupine quills, her tail shot up, and with a hiss that was anything but friendly, Tejas disappeared under the pleated flounce of our orange couch.

As I stooped to retrieve her, Byzie, seated in his brown tweed recliner, spoke up. "Leave her alone. Let her hide. She's had a big shock."

I straightened and looked at him, trying not to notice how his stocky body was slumped to one side in the chair. Or how his dark brown hair had grayed almost overnight. And those bright blue eyes that had stolen my heart twenty-five years before—how could his pain darken them so much?

I quickly turned my face away. "All right, honey, I'll leave old scaredy-cat alone." I was relieved to hear the steadiness in my voice as I flashed the bright smile I was trying to perfect. "I'm sure she'll adjust."

But she didn't. In the days that followed, Tejas crept out only to eat or use the litter box when no one was around. The rest of us were almost as timid, afraid to upset Byzie in his brown tweed recliner. There was no discussion about the "problem."

Alan and Kristan retreated more and more to their rooms. Byzie seldom left his chair. The "cave" under the orange couch became Tejas's permanent home. And I felt like climbing into bed, pulling the covers over my head, and not coming out myself. I was finding it increasingly difficult to be "up" all the time, but I kept trying. I just had to keep the family happy.

One day, returning from the grocery store, I was astonished to find Byzie in the den with the kitten draped across his right shoulder. "Look, hon, I'm petting Tejas!"

Everything on Tejas was flat. Her hair, her ears, even her tail—swishing like an angry snake. Her eyes were narrow green slits. And I too felt upset. Why couldn't Byzie have left well enough alone?

"Byzie, she's scared. And furious. Please let her go."

A light snapped off in Byzie's eyes. He released the kitten, and in seconds she was back under the sofa. And Byzie returned to his chair.

Six days later I drove Byzie to the hospital. "The surgery will be minor," the doctor said. "Just the removal of scar tissue. But I'm concerned about your husband's depression."

After they rolled Byzie away, I sat waiting in his room, thinking about what the doctor said. There was a knock on the door. "Come in," I said reluctantly.

The hospital chaplain introduced himself. I took little note of his name, but I remember his handshake. Instead of one hand, he used two, clasping my hand in both of his and pressing gently. "How are you?" His voice seemed to fill the tiny room.

"I'm just fine," I said brightly.

"Just fine?"

"Yes, thank you." *I wish he'd leave*, I was saying to myself.

But he didn't. He squeezed my hand again and wouldn't let go. I looked at his shoes. He needs to polish that right one; it's scuffed. . . .

"Mrs. Parr." His voice softened. "I feel that in spite of what you're saying, you are not fine."

The part of me that was denying his words wanted to kick his left shoe and scuff it too; the part of me that was struggling for serenity clutched at what he was saying.

"Your life has changed dramatically," the chaplain said. "Please, ask God to help you accept that. There's a special kind of healing in acceptance. It gives you the strength to go on—in a new direction."

He continued to hold my hand as he prayed a short prayer, then he was gone.

I pulled Byzie's robe from the bed, bunched it in my arms and hugged it. *Oh, God,* I prayed, *I just can't keep avoiding the truth. I'm so tired of pretending that nothing's changed in our lives. Please help me.*

The intercom squawked. "Mrs. Parr, your husband is in recovery." As the doctor had expected, the surgery had been uneventful. That evening a drowsy Byzie urged me to go home.

When I arrived, Alan and Kristan were watching television. "How's Dad?" they asked, jumping up.

"He's just fine," I began. Then I remembered my prayer. Snapping off the TV, I sat down between them on the orange couch. "That is, the operation went all right, and he'll be home soon." I took a deep breath. "But he's sad about not being able to work anymore. I'm sad for him. And for us. I know both of you are too."

For the first time, I had removed my cheerful mask. My expression, my words, the tone of my voice, all reflected exactly how I was feeling. The children looked at me. Then, almost simultaneously, their tense faces and postures began to relax.

"Things aren't ever going to be like they used to be, are they, Mom?" I could see the glint of tears in Kristan's eyes.

"No, honey, they aren't."

"Is Dad going to die?" Alan repeated the question

he'd asked several times before. But this time, Alan got an honest answer.

"I don't know, son. We have to take one day at a time."

Suddenly I heard an annoyed hiss. My foot had brushed against the pleated flounce, and Tejas was letting us know she didn't want us bothering her. She wanted to hide, undisturbed, nothing changing, cowering in her cave.

"You want to know something, kids?" I said suddenly. "Just because things will never be like they used to be doesn't mean they can't be good—just different."

While the children looked at me in astonishment, I bent over, lifted the couch's flounce, and made an announcement. "Your life is going to be different too, Miss Scaredy-Cat Tejas," I called. "We're through hiding, and so are you!"

When Byzie came home from the hospital, we lifted the flounce on the orange couch and pinned it so that it would stay up. Soon Byzie helped us put a string on a plastic toy, and we started taking turns dragging it back and forth in front of the opening.

Gradually Tejas ventured out—first her head, then her front paws, finally all of her. Then, as we pulled the toy, she chased it madly around the room. Then up the den steps. Then into the kitchen. And into every room of her new home.

It seemed our whole family finally let out a collective sigh of relief. In the days and weeks that followed, we began discussing the changes in our lives openly and honestly. We all talked about the fears we had, the worry we felt, the adjustments we'd have to make. There was no more pretending or avoiding—just realistic talk about day-to-day changes. Changes that are still going on in our lives—and probably always will.

Today the orange couch and the brown tweed recliner are still in our home. But nobody's hiding, under or in them. And that scaredy-cat Tejas? She spends most of her time looking for a lap to sit on, now that she's such a friendly cat and all.

Two Days
and Three Cats

Caroline Miller

When fifteen-year-old Adam arrived at our house that winter day, I knew right away he was going to be more of a challenge than the first two troubled teens we had hosted. Even though his head was down and his shoulders slumped, there was an air of defiance about him. Adam responded with grunts when introduced to my thirteen-year-old son, Rick, and our cats. Dropping his bags on the bedroom floor, he crawled onto the bed and stared out the window.

After my husband's death and my oldest son's departure to college three years before, my two remaining kids and I had decided to make use of the extra bedroom by signing on with a local social service agency. We took in teenagers needing a place to stay for short periods while they were working out difficult family situations. Our first two placements had been fun and rewarding for us all. By the time Adam arrived, my daughter had gone off to college also, leaving just Rick, me, and our three cats at home.

As I made supper I mentally reviewed what the agency had told me about Adam. He felt he was being pushed out of his mother's life, unwanted, ever since she had remarried.

When his mother gave birth to a boy, Adam had become withdrawn. His stepfather was a nice guy, so Adam turned his anger and frustration inward. His home and school life became a disaster.

When dinner was ready I knocked on his door. No response. After knocking again, I peeked inside. Adam was lying on top of the bedspread, eyes open, bags still packed, and no lights on. He didn't reply to "Dinner is ready," so I put on a lamp and left him alone. After dinner I checked again, but nothing had changed except that one of the cats was lying next to Adam on the bed.

"Adam, you must be hungry. Can I bring you a sandwich?"

He nodded.

Just before retiring I looked in on him again. He was still rooted to the bed with the cat, but the sandwich and milk were gone. *Maybe things will be better tomorrow*, I thought.

They weren't. The only change was that a different cat had joined Adam on the bed. He shook his head at my attempts to get him up for school.

I can outlast him, I thought determinedly. *I'll win him over yet!* I brought him juice and toast for breakfast. No comment, no acknowledgment, but the plate and glass were empty a few hours later.

I began to get concerned and a little bit angry that afternoon when there was still no change. Nonetheless, the cats continued taking turns on the bed with him. They seemed enchanted with him.

That evening Rick's youth group met at church, which included dinner. I had planned to stay with him since it was my turn to wash dishes. When I asked Adam to come along, he shook his head. Wearily I made him another sandwich and left it along with some cookies and milk.

In the car on the way to church Rick asked, "How long is Adam going to stay with us?"

"After I call the agency tomorrow, they'll probably pick him up. I think he's past any help we can give him."

Rick was silent for a moment, then said, "I think Adam deserves the same consideration we gave Andre."

"The cat?" I asked, dumbfounded. "What do you mean by that?"

"Remember how when we adopted Andre a couple of years ago you put food and water out and told us kids to leave him alone; he would come to us when he was good and ready?" Rick continued. "It seems fair to give Adam the same consideration as the cat. It's been only two days, and it took the cat four or five before he came around."

I had to admit he had a point. "Okay, we'll give Adam a few more days to get used to us," I reassured Rick.

At church Rick asked the youth leader to pray for Adam. I began to dread what we would find at home. But when we walked through the door, Adam was sitting on the couch, eating an apple and watching television as if he had been a member of our household for years.

"I hope it's okay that I took a shower and put away my clothes," he said.

Within the week, Adam opened up. He returned to school and did his homework. Soon he and Rick were like brothers. And at least one of the cats slept on his bed at night.

A week before Adam was to return home, the placement agency called. "Adam's psychologist said he's ready to go home now," the woman informed me. "She said he must have been with a special family."

"Yep," I told her, "around here we treat kids every bit as well as we do our cats."

Cat With No Name

Bert Clompus

T he cat showed up a few days after my bookkeeper, Norman, told me he was quitting. Scrawny as a frayed piece of rope and gray as a foggy morning, she sat high atop a bale of hay in my barn, mewing and complaining. That reminded me of how Norman had reacted when I tried handing him a key to my hardware store so he could open up in the morning. "I'm quitting, Bert. I can't handle that responsibility right now," he complained. I looked at my employee's pallid face and frowned. He disappointed me and I told him so. But I excused him from opening up the store and let him get back to his bookkeeping.

I wish I could have ignored Norman's refusal the way I ignored the gray cat. I busied myself filling three bowls for the cats I already had—Faith, Hope, and Sheldon. When I was finished, the gray cat jumped to the floor, boldly pushed Sheldon aside, and began eating his food. Sheldon, who was twice her size, looked up at me and protested. "Hey," I told him. "I can't fight your battles."

The gray intruder quickly finished Sheldon's food and shouldered Faith aside to get at hers. "I bet I know where you come from," I accused. "You come from that cat-infested old barn down the road."

I didn't need another cat. So after she was finally satisfied, I opened the barn door and shouted, "Shoo!" But the gray cat ignored me and nonchalantly climbed back on the bale of hay. That irritated me almost as much as Norman's refusal to take the key.

The next morning the gray cat was still there, staring down at me and informing me how hungry she was. "That's tough," I snapped. I filled my cats' dishes, put them outside the barn, and left. Later, I saw she was outside, pushing my cats aside and attacking their food. And one by one my cats walked away, totally disgusted with her, as I was with Norman.

When the pushy feline finished eating, she tried making friends with my cats. She began rubbing against them, but they either walked away or batted her with their paws. I didn't blame them. Then I—and my sixty-seven-year-old temper— picked up a stone and hurled it at her. The cat scooted around the side of the barn.

Immediately I became guilt-ridden and hoped God was busy looking somewhere else. I also hoped it was the last I had seen of the little pest. But the object of my short-lived wrath cautiously peeked at me from the corner of the barn. "Okay, have it your way," I muttered. It was the same thing I had muttered to Norman.

The following morning the gray cat was first to greet me and begin her incessant chatter as she followed me into the barn. There she watched me fill the bowls. There were four now, and she hungrily tore into them. When Faith, Hope, and Sheldon finally arrived I had to put more food in the dishes. "Keep this up and you'll eat me out of house and home!" I complained to the gray cat, who contentedly licked her paws. It reminded me of the way Norman had contentedly returned to his quiet world of bookkeeping for me.

However, I soon began looking forward to the gray cat's early-morning greetings down by the hydrant outside the barn. And one morning, while I was retrieving the empty bowls, she quickly rubbed the back of my hand with her cheek and dashed away. It happened faster than the beat of a butterfly wing. A few days later she allowed me to pet her and, finally, hold her. She weighed next to nothing. That cat and Norman were really two of a kind. "Dear Lord," I prayed, "help me put some meat on this poor thing."

Faith, Hope, and Sheldon continued to snub the gray cat, which made me more sympathetic toward her. I decided to have my vet check her out. I also intended to have her spayed. The vet told me to put her in a carrier the night before her operation.

When that night arrived, I tried putting her into the carrier, but she seemed to have grown another four legs. It was like fighting a furry octopus. She also began mewing pitifully, as though knowing what lay ahead for her. Her cries broke my heart and made me relax my grip. She got free and disappeared into the night. "Good!" I shouted after her. "I'll never see you again, and things will get back to normal around here!"

The following morning, much to my relief, she was waiting at the hydrant. I bent down to pet her, but she would have none of it. She ate with one eye on her food and one eye on me. And for good reason too—the next time I would show no mercy, and off to the vet she would go.

But my plans for the gray cat evaporated like rain on a hot sidewalk. She was finally putting on weight, but it was all in her belly. After a few days, it became obvious she was pregnant, and I knew then why she had pushed her way into my life. I only wished I knew why gentle Norman had failed me.

"Boy, you sure know how to complicate things around here," I complained to the gray cat. I was certain this would be the last straw for Faith, Hope, and Sheldon, and they would pack up and leave. Nevertheless, I tried building up the pregnant cat for her coming ordeal by feeding her as much as she could consume.

The day finally came when the gray cat gave birth to three kittens in one of the stalls. Two were alive. One was gray and striped like a tiger. The other was carbon-black from the tip of its nose to the tip of its tail.

The kittens remained in the stall for a few more days and then disappeared. I looked everywhere for them, but couldn't find them. I wondered if their mother had done away with them. "Where are they?" I demanded when she showed up for her evening meal. The tired cat looked at me a second then quietly ate her food. I decided the babies were really gone and became very angry. "Okay, kitty-cat, no babies, no special treatment!" I told her, and gave her less food the next day.

But that old guilt hit me again. What if she were still feeding them somewhere? And aside from that, she was becoming so emaciated it was painful to look at her. She reminded me of Norman, who was steadily losing weight and looking so fragile he could break in half.

A week later she was in the barn waiting for me to fill her dish when something caught my eye. It was a little black head peering at me from a crack between two bales of hay. I froze and waited. A little gray head appeared too. I looked at their weary mother and shamefully conceded, "I guess I had no faith in you. I hope you'll accept my apology." I said nearly the same thing to Norman when I finally learned his sister had been stricken with Alzheimer's the year before, and he had been exhausting himself caring for her.

Each day I watched the gray cat pull her kittens toward her to feed them. I don't know how she did it. She became thinner and thinner, and I prayed for the day her babies would be weaned so she could rest.

Then, one day, the kittens began eating food from their mother's bowl, and the next morning the gray cat wasn't waiting at the hydrant for me. When she finally showed up she was breathing strangely and wouldn't eat. She just rested a while in the sun and then disappeared. It worried me more when she didn't show up for her evening meal. I put a bowl of food in the barn for the kittens and kept them company while they ate.

While I watched the kittens, the gray cat appeared. She rubbed against my leg as she walked slowly past me. Her eyes a bit out of focus and breathing with great difficulty, she lay down and seemed to wait. I petted her while the kittens lay next to her. Then I left them alone together.

The next morning I took a shirt from my closet and carried a shovel down to the barn, where I found what I knew I would find. I wrapped the gray cat in my shirt and buried her next to the stream winding through my property. Then I prayed the Twenty-third Psalm and, as though she could still hear me, whispered, "I loved you, gray cat."

Right then it struck me hard that I had never given her a name. I ran back to the barn and picked up her two babies. "Your name is Tiger," I told the striped kitten. "And your name is Hoppy," I said to the black one, who had a funny little walk.

As they scampered away, I thought about the gray cat, who, like Norman, I had condemned before knowing the facts. I closed my eyes and promised God I would try breaking my awful habit of jumping to conclusions. Then I thanked him for Norman, and for the kittens who now greet me down at the hydrant the way their mother had.

Babe in the Woods

Shari Smyth

Y ou know what's missing?" I said to my husband, Whitney. It was a warm evening, and the two of us were lounging on our long, low front porch, looking out over the yard. Our cats, Sheba and Bucci, played at our feet.

"I can't imagine," Whitney said, loafers propped on a stool.

"The kids," I said. "I wish they could pop in for dinner."

"Well, they can't. They live too far away."

"What I meant was—"

"I know what you meant," he interrupted, moving closer. "We've had this conversation before. You want our kids to move here to Tennessee. Having them so far away worries you."

"It does," I said. I had never gotten used to being a long-distance mom.

Our son, Jon, lived in Maine. Recently he'd gone camping in the northern part of the state and was supposed to have returned two days earlier. We hadn't heard from him. Every time I called I got the message on his answering machine: "Can't come to the phone right now." I worried something might have happened to him.

When I'd last spoken to our daughter Wendy, she was

160

upset because she'd just broken up with her boyfriend. "I really need a hug from you, Mom," she'd told me on the phone. I wished I could hop into the car and get to her, but Hawaii was a long drive from Tennessee.

And Sanna was in Florida and Laura was all the way in Oregon. Sure, they had jobs and friends. They phoned and even visited once in a while. Still I worried, and it was hard to know if my prayers for them had any effect.

"They're good kids," Whitney reminded me. "They can take care of themselves. You need to accept that."

"Easy for you to say. You're not their mother," I retorted as the phone rang.

I dashed into the house to answer it, tripping over the cats' food dish on the way. It was Jon. "Hey, Mom. Camping was great. I got back a few days ago. Sorry I forgot to call."

"I was worried," I said, an edge to my voice.

"Mom, I can take care of myself. Honest," he replied.

Can he really? Sighing, I returned to the porch. I reached for the cats' food dish at the top of the steps but froze when I noticed something lurking in the bushes. A scrawny calico cat looked out from the branches, staring at the food, whiskers twitching.

"It's all right," I said softly, setting down the dish and backing into the house. I watched through the window. The cat crept up the steps and peered around, a hunted, haunted look on her face. Her dull coat stretched taut over her jutting bones. She devoured the food, then took off. The next night she returned, and the next, and the one after that.

"We have a new cat," I told Whitney. "I've named her Babe."

He laughed. "I hope she lets you know where she is after dark."

The fifth night it was raining. When the cat poked her head above the steps, I was waiting. In the dry shelter of the porch, I'd placed a bed of towels and a dish of tuna. "Come here, Babe," I coaxed. "I won't hurt you." She crept toward the food, fur standing almost straight up. Stretching her neck, she began to nibble. Gingerly I scratched the wet fur between her ears. She stiffened, then relaxed. *Whitney was right,* I thought. *Now I have someone else to worry about.*

During the next few weeks reports came in from the kids: Laura was fighting a cold. Sanna was having roommate problems. Wendy had a date with a new guy. And I had Babe. She came daily, eating from the dish of food I put out. Her calico coat thickened and began to shine. She stretched out on the wooden porch, falling asleep on her back. I planned to take her to the vet to get fixed, but one autumn day she didn't show up for her usual meal. I drove around looking for her. I hiked, checking the woods. I left food out all night. When it remained untouched, I imagined the worst.

As Christmas approached I had to put Babe out of my mind. My children were coming home! For the first time in two years I had all four of them under one roof. They filled the house with good news: Laura had a steady beau. Sanna and Jon had both gotten promotions. Wendy had a new cottage overlooking the ocean. And for a whole glorious week, I wasn't a long-distance mom.

One night at dinner I ventured, "Why don't you all consider relocating to Tennessee? Dad and I can help with the move and finding jobs. You could live here till you found a place." Forks clattered to the table, and everyone fell silent.

Finally Sanna spoke, "Maybe someday, Mom. But for now we're happy where we are."

By week's end the kids had all gone. The house felt empty. And whenever I stepped onto the porch, there was no calico cat sneaking in from the woods to feast at the food dish. All I had for my children, and that undomesticated cat, were my prayers—and worries.

Then, on a raw, wet, late-March evening, I found Babe huddled on the porch mat. I was thrilled to see her, until I took a closer look. Her coat was dull and scraggly. She was pregnant, and obviously due any day. "You poor thing," I said, stroking her gently. She mewed meekly.

I fed her, toweled her off, and lined a waterproof crate with throw rugs. "There's your nursery," I informed her. Babe sniffed the crate and curled up inside it. I stood watching her, feeling nervous like an expectant grandmother.

On April Fool's Day I opened the door to find a newly sleek Babe. "Congratulations, Mama. Where's your brood?" But the joke was on me. I looked in the crate. Empty. I shined a flashlight under the porch. No kittens. I looked everywhere. "Where are they?" I fretted as I brought Babe her breakfast. She ate, washed herself, then stretched out to nap. I went inside. When I came out a minute later, Babe was gone.

I called the vet. "I have to find those kittens before something happens to them!"

"You might as well give up," he said. "It's out of your control. Trust her instincts."

Fat chance, I thought. I tramped through the woods. I looked under logs, in a woodpile, in an old, abandoned shed. I rooted through piles of dead leaves. Turkey vultures circled high above me. I shuddered to think what might have happened.

Yet in the following weeks, every morning Babe continued to come by for breakfast, then slip away. While she ate I worried about those kittens. *What was I going to do? Hadn't I tried everything?* Babe washed her whiskers and her ears, looking at me sideways. "Trust her instincts," the vet had said.

Suddenly it seemed so simple. Trust. That was the one thing I hadn't tried. Trust Babe. Trust my children. Trust God.

One day Jon called. "Guess what, Mom? The guys and I are planning a trip to India. We're going to quit our jobs and go for two months."

I gripped the counter, picturing my son lost in Calcutta, all his money spent. *Trust, Shari. Trust.* When I opened my mouth, I heard myself say, "This is the time of life to do those things . . . before you settle down and have a family."

There was a stunned silence at the other end of the line. Then, "Thanks, Mom. I was kind of dreading telling you." I think I surprised Jon as much as I surprised myself.

Speaking of surprised, on a balmy May afternoon I opened the door and there was Babe with three adorable, orange tabby kittens. Mama looked up at me with a cat grin that said, "Here they are, all healthy." Three boys I named Billy, Bobby, and Tommy. They live with their mom on my porch.

"Just wait till we show up with kids someday," Sanna joked. I'm waiting, peacefully for once, trusting God.

The Cat in the Conspiracy

Aletha Lindstrom

O*nly eight o'clock and already this house is like an oven,* I thought irritably. Setting my coffee cup on the kitchen counter, I reached across the sink to close the shutters against the intense July heat. Just before they clicked shut, I glimpsed some small animal moving along a fencerow in the far pasture. A cat.

Another animal dumped, I decided—and felt a rush of anger at callous pet owners who abandon unwanted cats and dogs along country roads. But the incident was soon forgotten, swallowed by a deeper anger that had been seething inside me since an argument with my husband Andy the night before.

It was one of those times when he took charge of decision-making in a way that made me feel my own opinion and role in the matter were belittled. Or so it seemed to me. I'd responded sarcastically in a way well-calculated to wound his pride. He'd made an angry reply. And so it built until we thoroughly disliked each other.

By bedtime we weren't speaking, and the silence continued through breakfast. I remembered the set look on his face as he shoved his chair away from the table, grabbed his briefcase, and stalked silently out the door. Not one word of apology. Not even a goodbye.

This hadn't happened before in our twenty years of marriage. Like all husbands and wives, we exchanged occasional sharp words, but never had our anger lasted this long. And never had I felt so humiliated, so rejected. I refused to consider that Andy's usual good humor had been sabotaged by hot, sleepless nights—and by eight hours of daily sweltering in an office without air-conditioning. I refused to consider that I, too, was extremely edgy from a week of record-breaking temperatures.

Instead, I nursed my grievance. "He'll probably come home expecting all to be forgiven and forgotten," I muttered. My bitter mood intensified as I cleared away coffee cups, untouched toast, and bowls of half-eaten cereal. I lifted Andy's chair to replace it by the table. Suddenly I felt an urge to retaliate. "Well, it won't be forgotten! I'm tired of being treated like a child!" I slammed the chair down. "Maybe I won't even be here!" I said. "Let him find out how it feels to be walked out on!"

The boldness of the idea frightened me. Yet I felt determined—and strangely exhilarated. Where could I go? To relatives? To a motel? I'd have to think about it. Then some inner voice warned: *Get out of the house. Take a walk. Consider this carefully before you do something you'll regret!* I glanced at the clock. Eight-thirty. I still had plenty of time.

My energy, fueled by my need to get even, propelled me rapidly down the country road. The sun burned through my thin blouse, but I was more aware of the resentment simmering inside me. As I walked along, kicking angrily at stones, I dredged up old hurts and insults, building my case for leaving.

I'd covered about a half-mile when, for the first time, I noticed my surroundings. A farmhouse, vacant for several weeks, stood near the road. I often passed it when I drove into town. Now the dense shade of an ancient maple tree by the front porch proved irresistible.

I sank onto the bottom porch step and dropped my head to my arms. *If I'm going to get away by noon, I'd better get packed*, I thought.

Then I heard a faint, questioning "Meow?" and looked down to see a small white cat. Was it the animal I'd seen earlier along the fencerow? Probably. Foraging. By the looks of its emaciated little body, it hadn't had much success. For a moment I forgot my self-pity. "Why, you poor half-starved creature," I exclaimed. "I'll bet they moved out and left you!"

The scrawny kitten leaped on the step and tried to crawl into my lap. Instantly I regretted my words of concern. *I'll have trouble shaking her*, I thought in exasperation. I stood up and hurried out of the yard. But she came tumbling after me, crying, circling my feet, trying to rub against my legs.

I stopped. She sat down in front of me, looking up into my face. "Now, listen, cat," I said firmly. "We don't need a cat. I don't want a cat. So, scram! Get lost!" Her gaze never wavered.

I was about to pick her up and drop her over the fence into a cornfield when a large truck came bearing down on us, traveling much too fast for a country road. It thundered by, and when the dust cleared, the cat was gone, apparently terrified into headlong flight.

I walked back along the road, still brooding about leaving. Before I reached home, an idea came to me. We owned a cabin on a lake about four hours north. No telephone. No mail service. I'd just pack and go there. And I wouldn't leave a note for Andy. At first he'd think I'd gone on an errand. But when I hadn't returned by nightfall, he'd look in the bedroom closet and find my bag missing. He might do some calling around; then he'd probably conclude I'd gone to the cabin. But he wouldn't know for sure. He'd be angry—and worried. *Well, let him worry*, I thought grimly. *When he's concerned enough, he'll come after me. And he can apologize.*

I had nearly finished packing when that inner voice accosted me again: *What if he doesn't come after you? What if he won't apologize? He has a lot of pride, you know.*

Well, I was proud too! Still, in spite of the heat, I felt a chill of apprehension. I couldn't recall ever going out, even on an errand, without leaving a note saying when I'd be back. And what if he didn't come after me? Would I come crawling home? Would this resentment remain, like an ugly, unhealing wound, between us? We loved each other deeply. But we had friends our age who'd loved each other, too, until an act of rejection, like the one I contemplated, became the first step toward separation—and eventual divorce.

Again I probed for the hurt inside me. It was still there. I felt my cheeks burn with anger, and the apprehension died. I zipped my bag firmly shut and hurried into the hall and out the back door.

My car, thank goodness, was filled with gas. I tossed my bag on the rear seat and backed out of the garage. Then I glanced at the seat beside me. The local newspaper I'd bought the day before lay there. By chance—or maybe it wasn't chance—I'd left it in the car when I'd carried the groceries into the house. Now one of the headlines on the front page caught my eye: *Boy Scouts Sponsor "Be Kind to Animals" Program.* Be kind to animals. The words seemed to leap out at me.

Animals? The cat! I'd completely forgotten her! Now the memory of the small, helpless creature tugged at me. And for the second time that day, I forgot my self-pity. How could I have been so heartless? "Inasmuch as ye have done it unto one of the least of these . . ." (Matthew 25:40). Did God mean cats too? I had no choice. I had to go back. And, remembering how the truck frightened her, I decided to walk.

"She's just a tramp," I told myself. "She'll be long gone by now—and I can leave with a clear conscience."

But she wasn't gone. When I approached the cornfield, she came bounding out, as if she'd been expecting me. And perhaps she had. She followed me home and into the kitchen.

I warmed milk for her and cut up some leftover chicken. "Go ahead, eat," I said, placing the food on the floor. I expected she'd gulp it ravenously like most hungry animals. I was wrong. As I turned to the refrigerator, I heard that same faint, questioning "Meow?" I looked down. She sat at my feet, her little face raised to mine.

"You've got food," I said in exasperation. "No self-respecting cat turns down chicken."

She raised a paw and timidly touched my leg. "Meow," she cried again.

"What is it?" I said, picking her up. She nestled close to me, purring ecstatically, then rubbed her head against my cheek. Finally, she settled contentedly against my neck, singing that ridiculous little song.

So that was what she wanted! Love. Unbelievably, it was more important to that starving cat than food or drink. Love. The basic need of all God's creatures. Including me. *Including Andy*, I thought with a pang.

I placed the cat by her food and stroked her gently while she gobbled the chicken and lapped the milk. And I thought back through the previous afternoon and through the morning. That inner voice, the walk, the newspaper headline, the cat—all working together to keep me from leaving. Was it a conspiracy? Suddenly I knew it was. God's conspiracy. Long ago I'd learned he sometimes uses unusual channels to save us from self-destruction.

I breathed a sigh of thanks. Then I remembered something I'd forgotten. No matter how good a marriage is, there are bound to be times of bitterness, of dissension, of wanting to "get even." The marriage vow is "for better, for worse," and we all need to build reserves of kindness and forgiveness to help us through the bad times. Because, as the little cat had just reminded me, love is by far the most important thing we have.

Stroking the soft fur, I searched once again for the angry resentment inside me. It was gone. The cat had finished eating, so I picked her up. Looking into her eyes, I said, "Andy doesn't like cats." She yawned, showing her pink little tongue. "But I love you," I added, "so he'll love you too. He's that kind of guy."

Part of

the Family

Checkered Past

Marianna K. Tull

I grew up in a simpler time and in a simpler place than our world is now, on a seventy-five-acre farm with many animals. It's the cats I remember most.

When I was five, Calico peeked out of my dad's overcoat pocket one evening upon his return from work, and I stared back with wide, eager eyes. She taught me how to love and be loved in return.

When I was a young girl, I opened the door for a scrawny little stray who was begging to be part of our lives. Tigger called forth from me pity and compassion. Later, when he became big and strong and the mighty hunter of our farm, spurning the front door to enter and exit boldly through the windows, he showed me how exciting it was to grow and change.

Tigger's proudest moment came the day he caught his first field mouse, hopped up on his accustomed windowsill and tried to utter his loudest "Please let me in!" What a decision! A very loud meow would let the mouse escape and dash his hopes of displaying his hunting prowess. With quiet humility, he would have his mouse but no one would ever see it. Growing into a mighty hunter wasn't going to be easy!

Luckily for Tigger, my mother passed the window, praised him for his skill, but let him know the mouse was not welcome in the house.

Tigger could be a gentle friend too. My mighty hunter let me tie a baby bonnet under his chin and wheel him around in my doll buggy.

When I left the farm and became a mother, I thought I had left my cats and the lessons of my childhood behind forever. I had a life to build and sons to raise and so many new challenges on my mind. But as my sons grew, they let me know that parakeets, rabbits, gerbils, and even a dog weren't enough. A cat had to be part of the family.

Blackie was a bold windowsill jumper. He never failed to appear on our neighbor's kitchen sill whenever the aroma of cooking liver assailed his pink nose.

Marmalade could be a fireball of energy when my youngest son wanted him to be. But he was happiest draped around my boy's neck as a huge, yellow fur piece, both of them quietly content.

Now that I am almost seventy-five, I find myself remembering the farm in greater clarity, like an old painting I have returned to, seeing fresh strokes of color. It is Checkers who stands out in sharpest relief.

He was huge and sleek with a startling black-and-white fur coat. He shared my grandmother's home, and they were indeed two of a kind. Both were very independent but easy to love and admire. I think Checkers enjoyed as many privileges as we, her grandchildren, did. His upholstered chair in the living room was a sight to see. One side was almost totally destroyed—his claw sharpener! He shared her bed, but never until the room was dark. Then he would stretch himself out full length, back-to-back with his loving mistress. The house they shared was a restored nineteenth-century stone farmhouse with a rather unusual water system. The water was pumped by a hydraulic ram from a spring in the meadow to an enormous wooden storage tank in the attic. From there it ran by gravity to the kitchen and bathroom of my grandmother's house.

One night, my grandmother was awakened by Checkers's loud meowing beside her bed. After several admonishments did not succeed in silencing him, my grandmother followed him groggily into the hallway. Checkers ran immediately to the attic door, meowing loudly and pawing frantically at the door. Totally mystified and just a little annoyed, my grandmother opened the door and nipped the switch, flooding the attic steps with light. Just beginning to cascade down the steps was a very healthy stream of water, overflowing from the storage tank! A hasty call to my father, and the pump was shut off, preventing a disastrous flood. With crisis solved, Checkers sauntered back to the bedroom with his usual airy confidence, his detached mood indicating "It's all in a night's work." Ever after, I felt I should curtsy to him in deference to his uncanny knowledge of disaster looming on the horizon. Who knew what Checkers's next move would be?

When I sit at my typewriter, I try not to let Sparky, my amour of the moment, read this; and I silently mouth my apologies to all the other very intelligent and loving furry critters who have brightened my days. Sparky thinks she is the only feline who has ever shared my love and my life. She knows nothing of a ten-year-old girl who lived on a farm with many animals, and a cat named Checkers who taught her that life was a difficult challenge and a foreboding journey; but there was tenderness and courage and mystery and quiet bliss with our feline friends to share the way.

Amber

Gladys Taber

Recently I read that there are ten million cats in the United States, which means five million more cats than dogs. I always wonder how experts arrive at these round figures. Even as they estimate, more puppies are turning blind noses to the daylight and thimble-sized kittens are reaching for the first mouthful of warm, life-giving milk. So who knows?

But the preponderance of cats does suggest that a cat can take care of himself better than a dog. A cat can pry open a garbage can and fish out something or sneak in an alleyway and find a mouse or rat. A homeless dog either starves or gets run over or shot by some ambitious hunter. In the city, a cat can jump from one apartment-house roof to another. A dog cannot even get up there. Also, a chased cat can vanish as no dog can. In my part of the country, an unlicensed dog is picked up and, if no home is found, is destroyed. But nobody pays any attention to the cats that live off the land and do not wear licenses.

The country cats that visit my yard would never submit to a collar and license. Sometimes I wonder what would happen if cats had to have licenses—spayed females so much, altered males so much, unspayed females more, etc. I would very much like to have Amber registered at the Town Hall and listed with a number and my address, but I realize wearing a small metal tag would drive her crazy.

It would also, again, involve a collar to hang the license on. A harness would be useless because when the harness is used, the owner is there. Recently I met a charming golden retriever puppy shipped from Canada and he had a serial number for identification tattooed on one ear.

But a golden has firm thick ears, whereas no cat has ears thick enough to tattoo. And the golden could not tell me whether this hurt a good deal at the time or not. It is, however, a permanent insurance against anyone stealing a valuable dog, whereas dog stealers toss collars away as they go about their business of marketing stolen dogs.

So far, I cannot think of any way to attach a label and phone number to a cat!

Advertisements for lost dogs usually give the license number, but advertisements for lost cats are pathetic. "Lost in the vicinity of ____, one spayed female with white paws and a white forefront. Answers to the name of Baby." Since Baby is not apt to rush up to a stranger, this is not very helpful.

Also cats do not identify so readily with a name. Amber comes when I call her either Amber or Sweetheart. But since she is nearly always underfoot, calling her is seldom necessary except when she gets shut in a closet. Then I wish that when I call "Amber" she would call back instead of just sitting in the dark and waiting.

Esme knew her name very well but paid no attention unless she was on her way already. And Tigger, the Manx, would turn his green-glass eyes to me and imply I was very silly because I could see him, couldn't I?

This curious indifference to a label may be peculiar to Amber. She understands very well when I say "Let's go for a walk." Or, "I have something for you to eat—come in the kitchen." Or, "I am going for the mail but I shall be right back." And she knows what the word *No* means. After one nibble of the best African violet, she waits for that "No."

I talk to her about everything and would advise any cat owner to do the same with his cat. Too many cat owners accept a cat's apparent indifference to special commands. Since I have lived with Amber, I know the variations in her voice and can understand almost everything she tries to tell me. I think this is reciprocal. Otherwise when I explain I am going to the typewriter to work, why does she fly ahead of me and jump on the machine and begin pushing the buttons to see the keys hop up?

And even when I don't talk to her, Amber understands what I am thinking. When I have to shut her in the bedroom preparatory to my going out, I have to sneak in and turn the rug back so the door will close. I try not to let her observe this tactic. If she sees me shove the rug over, she vanishes and I am late for the party because I can't find her.

"Well, this is a surprise," one friend said as I turned up ten minutes late for dinner, "you are always so early we just rush to get ready and even so we are always late. But here you are! Late."

"Amber didn't want to be left alone," I explained.

When I get back I call from the front door, "I'm back! Sweetheart!" She is at the door of the bedroom, yawning. She has been asleep on the pillow and probably hasn't missed me at all, but she is like an actor in the third act of a play. She rises to the drama of my coming home and not abandoning her forever. Jumping around, purring, kneading her paws, rubbing her head against my hand, twitching her tail, and putting an occasional melancholy *miaow* in the middle of a purr. She has, she implies, suffered excruciatingly.

Which brings me to the point of sleeping. A puppy who is left alone may yell his head off until his lips are foam-flecked. He may claw the door, tear up the furniture, and make a career of suffering. When he is older, he gets over this. A kitten goes to sleep. This is partly because cats sleep more than dogs. Recently I read another one of those doubtful statements to the effect that a cat may sleep seventeen hours a day.

If so, it is because a cat exercises violently and completely. The acrobatics of a kitten remind me of Ringling's circus. After Amber goes at a dizzying speed, up in the air, the whole length of the house, for half an hour, she takes a nap with paws folded under her chin, tail quiescent.

A hunting dog may run all day and after a brief rest be ready for an automobile ride. But he does not use every muscle in his body the way a cat does. He seldom leaps, climbs, swings in the air; he just runs through brush. This observation is purely my own without benefit of experts.

The agility of a kitten is amazing until you get used to it. I watch Amber and decide this is the nearest thing to flying without wings. Also, she uses a lot of energy washing, which involves one hind leg at an acute angle while she scrubs, the head swiveled completely while she works at her ears. Her muscles seem to be fluent. The one place she cannot reach is behind her head between the ears, so I give special attention to that and she thanks me with a large enthusiastic purr.

When Amber is asleep, she is motionless as a figurine. This interests me because the dogs always dreamed. Holly, the Irish, would twitch her paws as if she were running a race and often wag her plumed tail wildly. She was a happy dreamer. Amber is quiet as still water. I have been told that all mammals dream (and perhaps birds too) and that the mind is eased by working things out while we sleep. If this is so, I conclude that Amber keeps her dreams inside her mind without reacting physically. The absolute repose of a sleeping cat somehow eases the tensions of a watcher. Often I reach out and touch Amber to be sure she is still warmly alive.

Amber wakes instantly. She may yawn once widely and then she is leaping-active. My cockers and Irish yawned and stretched and yawned again with sleepy-lidded eyes. I belong to this type myself, for the first hour I am up is like being on a slow boat to China, as it were.

But one interesting thing about Amber's sleep is that the slightest sound alerts her. Occasionally I can tiptoe past a dog-tired dog, but if I get up noiselessly in the night for a drink of water, Amber is already on the bathroom bowl, leaning over the faucet to catch the first drip when I turn it on. And when I move silently to the wing at the Cape to work at the typewriter, I often think she is sound asleep on the bed. But when I get to the wing, she is already perched on the carriage of my machine.

Finally, as to sleep, cats like secret places sometimes. Dogs usually choose their own bed and never sleep anywhere else. But Amber may emerge from the linen closet or the kitchen cupboard. She has two kitten houses, one especially made by the grandchildren and one bought at a fancy pet store and equipped with a rug and an upper porch, but she almost never uses them. I have learned when I open a drawer never to close it entirely in case she has slipped in for a nap. Or I may find her tucked in the bookshelves, warmed by Keats and Shakespeare.

Once I closed the closet door in the wing and went peacefully to bed, assuming she was in the chair by the open fire. In the morning I called her and had no answer and began a frantic search. After combing the whole house, I opened that one closet door and out came Amber, a little cross at being confined in there all night but otherwise quite self-possessed. Now I leave that door ajar too, for her melancholy confinement did not give her a horror of the closet. It is full of fine things to play with, she says.

The one place where she never lies down is the right half of the best sofa. Even if I am sitting on that sofa at the other end, she leaps from the table to my side without invading the right end, which was Holly's. Since she never saw Holly, there can be no memory pattern, and certainly none of that sweet-hay scent of an Irish is left, so I am happy to assume that Amber has an understanding with Holly herself.

In our Connecticut house a lot has happened. The previous owner murdered his wife one night and then committed suicide, which must have been hard on their houseguest, who had come to the country to visit them after a nervous breakdown. My own feeling about the household ghosts is that they are companionable. They all, in their time, loved Stillmeadow. No matter what tragedies they endured, the fact that this house was cherished is evident in every hand-hewn stone and hand-cut beam. But I wondered about Amber who is so very sensitive.

At first when she heard footsteps and nobody was there, her ears went out like wind-blown sails. A ridge of fur rose along her backbone. Occasionally she uttered a faint hiss. But before long she was only curious and interested. Sometimes around two in the morning she stands on tiptoe at the foot of the old pineapple-post bed. She rests her triangle of chin on the footboard and stares wide-eyed through the bedroom door into the family room beyond. When the footsteps cease, she yawns and tucks up again on my pillow.

The only time she objected was one night when suddenly two books flung themselves from the top shelf in the bedroom. They were books dating back to 1800, bound in ancient leather. One was *Poems of Old Age* and one *Poems for a Young Man*. I have no idea whose they were in the beginning, but they landed on the maple daybed with muffled bangs, and Amber leaped six inches in the air.

Most of the animals that have owned me have had perceptions I could not have. When they prowl around nervously, I stop whatever I am doing and look to see what has gone wrong in the house. When they jump on the windowsill and look earnestly down the road, I take off my apron and powder my face hastily. Long before the sound of a motor is heard, they know. But if the car coming down the road is not going to stop at Stillmeadow or Still Cove, as the case may be, they pay no attention.

Amber, naturally, does not bark, but she is a good watcher. She jumps up and down, tail flashing back and forth. She unfurls her ears and points in the direction of the menace. If she hears the car of her favorite friend Margaret Stanger, she flies to the door, purring up a storm. Margaret always brings a snack. One time, though, she came directly from a party where she couldn't sneak even a morsel in her purse. Amber tried to open the purse, then went through the pockets of Margaret's sweater, and then sat down and miaowed pitifully. A week or so later, Margaret telephoned to say that she had started over to my house and got as far as the nearest neighbor's, but then realized she had forgotten Amber's snack so she turned around and went home.

This probably proves that a small kitten has no difficulty managing her subjects!

But I must add that the subjects are more flattered when she flies into their laps and spreads her paws and rubs her head against them and purrs and purrs than they would be if Queen Elizabeth awarded them something to hang around their necks.

Amber's self-appointed role as watchcat always surprises me. With Esme, the Siamese, her reaction to strangers at the door was to spin upstairs and hide in the bathroom. Tigger, the Manx, sat by the fire and scrubbed his blunt square face no matter who came in. But Amber hears a car coming far down the road. She always recognizes the sound of friends' cars, as I have said, although she had some trouble when Margaret bought a new one. The first time Margaret came in from that car Amber jumped on the harvest table and stared with disbelief. It took several minutes before she hurried over to say hello. The second or third time the car pulled in the drive, Amber was at the kitchen window waiting.

When a strange car turns down our road, Amber rushes to the front door and lashes her tail. If she thinks I have not noticed it—and I often haven't—she dashes in and jumps on my desk and then runs back to her watch-point.

Naturally she could never fall on an intruder and mangle him as a dog could. She cannot bark a warning. Even when she hisses you have to listen hard to hear her. But I feel perfectly secure with Amber to notify me someone is coming and which door he or she is coming toward and whether he or she is familiar or not. Furnace men, painters, electricians she greets with joy. But one night a strange man came to the door. He was trying to deliver a package from the next town and was hopelessly lost. Amber greeted his arrival like a miniature leopard (all five pounds of her).

No German shepherd could be a more dedicated guardian of the home than this small Abyssinian kitten.

The Cat Who Was Always There

Helena Marchant

Studzey was the stray who was always there, haunting our yard. Again and again he appeared out of the blue for a visit—but just to eat and run, never staying long. We never knew where he came from or where he was going. But one night, during a storm, Studzey came to us with a look in his eyes and a tilt to his head that seemed to say, "It's time."

My daughter saw his soaking fur coat and muddy paws and took pity. Studzey accepted her invitation inside and made himself quite comfortable that night—and the night after that. Maybe because he was a stray, he had the gift of never letting anything get in the way of what he needed—and it was a home he needed now.

After a few days, we realized happily that Studzey was ours for good. We had to officially adopt him and make a trip to the vet for neutering and a health check. It was then we learned that our Studzey had an advanced case of feline leukemia. The vet recommended we put him to sleep rather than go through an awful ordeal. Studzey had six months to live, perhaps less, the vet said. We were devastated. We had fallen in love with him, and he was already very much a part of our family.

I looked at Studzey. In his eyes I saw contentment, gentleness, and a sense of belonging. Studzey was three years old and probably a stray most of his life, the vet said. I thought, *how unfair for such a loving cat to have never known the warmth of a family.* That made the decision. The least we could do was give him a wonderful home for the last months of his life.

The vet recommended that he not be an outside cat anymore due to his illness. That was fine with us—and fine with Studzey. Our roaming tom suddenly had no desire to run out of the house even when a door was open. It was as though he had had enough of the cruel world out there and preferred the warmth of a home.

Whenever I looked up, Studzey was lounging on a sofa or bed. Seeking comfort, curling up against us wherever we were, purring away—these were his chief pleasures. He became our cat who was always there.

To our astonishment, Studzey breezed through the first six months. And the second six months. And six months after that. After three years of remarkable health, considering his disease, the vet was amazed. His only explanation was that Studzey was so happy and loved he managed to fight off the worst of his disease.

Every morning I would find him lying across my chest—almost as if he couldn't get close enough to me. When I would walk into the room, he would look up, and I would see what looked like a smile on his face with his eyes blinking constantly. If we watched TV, he'd jump on our laps and push his nose in our face, telling us that he wanted his head scratched. If you stopped scratching, he'd smack your chin with his paw to remind you to continue, please. Studzey always let us know he was there.

When I got ready for work, he'd bat my legs with his paws when I got out of the shower until I fed him. When we got home at the end of the day, Studzey would greet us and then follow us all over the house meowing loudly until we fed him—perhaps because we fed him salmon. And when he couldn't digest dry cat food, we discovered Studzey had a taste for chocolate chip ice cream. Studzey and I shared many a night watching a movie and enjoying our chocolate chip ice cream together. He was my baby, and I was so close to him.

When I brought home my future husband, there was Studzey giving him the once-over that first date and every date after that. My husband eventually got Studzey's final approval, and they became close friends.

Then one weekend, after three years, Studzey was so weak he could hardly move. The medication that had helped him with his various ailments didn't seem to be working anymore. He curled up on his favorite spot on the sofa and slept through the day, refusing to eat, even when I warmed his food to soothe his swallowing. When I petted him, he lifted his head and smiled, but I knew he didn't have much time. That night, I stayed with him for hours and said good-bye through my tears. I knew that I had to bring Studzey to the vet the next morning.

When I woke up, my husband told me that Studzey had peacefully passed away. God had made the decision for me. I was very upset, but then my husband told me the rest of his story.

He had gotten up early that Sunday morning, careful not to wake me because of the rough night I had with Studzey. He went outside to get the paper, stopping to check on Studzey, who'd spent the night on the sofa, too weak to climb upstairs. When he patted our kitty's head, Studzey lifted his head and purred. My husband talked to Studzey and patted him for a while before returning upstairs to me, quietly closing the door to read the paper.

A short time passed and my husband looked up from the paper and saw Studzey sitting there in front of him. He looked down at the paper but then suddenly realized that he had closed the door; how could Studzey have come into the room? When he looked again, Studzey was no longer there. He got up and looked at the door and it was still closed. Puzzled, he then went downstairs to check on Studzey, and it was then he found Studzey had passed away, lying so still on the sofa, still warm.

To this day, my husband believes that Studzey had come upstairs to say good-bye to him. After all, I had already said my good-byes to him the night before, but my husband hadn't. We miss Studzey very much. We are so grateful to have stolen four wonderful years with our cat who was always there.

Lovey

Betty Newsom

One summer my husband and I and our four children camped in our fold-down canvas-top camper in my parents' backyard for a few days. My mother warned me to keep my children away from a stray calico kitten because it was limping, and she was afraid it might be sick.

We placed our fold-out camper under an old apple tree next to my great grandparents' antique barn. The next morning we discovered that the little calico kitten, who limped and might be sick, had managed to climb up on the camper step, jump several inches up the metal side of the camper, wriggle under the snapped-down canvas wall, jump up, and curl up in bed beside three-year-old Kenny.

My husband and I carefully looked her over and decided she wasn't sick but just had a sore leg. Every night the small kitten found a way to climb into the camper and sleep next to Kenny. When we returned home, we took her with us.

I don't like to give a new animal a name until I'm sure it's not going to wander off, so some time went by before the little calico kitten received her name. One day, while I was folding clothes, I was thinking about a name for her and thought we might call her Lovey. Later that day, since the kitten had adopted Kenny, I asked him what he thought we should name her. I was surprised and pleased when he said "Lovey."

Of course, that became her name.

Lovey was a lot of company for Kenny when the older children went back to school. One afternoon, when she was almost full size, I looked out in the front yard and realized that there was something unusual about her that day— something quite different. Kenny had taken eight Band-Aids and stuck them all over her fur coat. I didn't know what might happen if Lovey tried to lick or scratch them off. I wasn't brave enough to go outside and start ripping Band-Aids off a cat, so before she could start trying to pick at them herself, I took my scissors outside and cut the hair underneath each Band-Aid and lifted them off. She went around looking like an awful "bad hair day" until all of her fur grew out to the same length again.

One day when I was alone in the house I heard a terrible commotion out in the garage. When I investigated the noise, I found Lovey howling and jumping around, trying to kill a fishing rod. Every time she jumped or hit it, the rod would slam against the wall. She must have tried to play with the fishing lure on the end of the line, and it had stuck in the bottom of her paw.

There are a lot of things that I wouldn't volunteer to do. Tackling an outraged cat, in severe pain, to remove a three-barbed fishing hook from her paw is high on my things-I-really-don't-want-to-do list. However, since I was the only person at home, it automatically became my job.

I wrestled Lovey into a bath towel with only her head and the harpooned paw sticking out. I placed her on the washer in her terry-cloth strait jacket. Talking very sweetly and confidently to her, I pried the hook out of her foot. She licked the paw clean and it didn't become infected. That evening I delivered a stern lecture to the boys about removing all lures and fish hooks from their lines before they put their fishing poles away.

A few years later we built a new house in my great-grandfather's woods, across the field behind my parents' home. Our calico cat, Lovey, had returned to her place of birth, but it wasn't an easy journey for her or for me. The day she returned to her birthplace, I fastened her in a box in the back seat of my station wagon. As I was driving down the road, she clawed her way out of the box and, terrified, agitated, and howling, she started bouncing off the seats and windows trying to escape. I drove very slowly the last five miles of the ten-mile ordeal, with Lovey clinging to the back of my seat, her front claws embedded in my neck and shoulders.

When we arrived at the woods I put her in a wire chicken pen under a big tree. She lived in the pen for three days until she calmed down. When she realized that all of our family was staying in this place and that this was now her home as well, we set her free. She was fine after that.

Time passed and Lovey became a mother. Our new house had a cement patio just outside the dining room door, and the dryer vent blew warm air out across it. During the cold months, Lovey and her kittens gathered at that corner of the patio and let the warm air blow over them. Even after the dryer had shut off, they would huddle together on top of the warm spot of cement.

It was a good arrangement for the adult cats, but unfortunately the little kittens liked it too. When the dryer was off, the kittens liked to crawl into the four inch aluminum exhaust pipe. As they grew bigger, they could no longer turn around to crawl out so they had to back out. They looked funny scooting out of the dryer vent backwards, decorated with lint fuzz.

I became concerned that some of them would get stuck in the pipe and we wouldn't be able to rescue them, so we placed a wire cover over the vent. That allowed the warm air to escape and eliminated the possibility of our kittens suffocating inside the narrow pipe, and it still allowed the cats their sauna-like experience on the patio.

Most cats seem to be instinctively drawn to dark, narrow places. We had a large stack of firewood by the barn that the kittens liked to climb on. When they were little they could crawl into some of the spaces between the chunks of wood to hide and take naps. As they grew bigger, they would sit and stare at the woodpile. They seemed to be trying to figure out why they could no longer jump into their kittenhood hiding places. The woodpile still looked the same as it always had to them. They just didn't realize they had outgrown the small, cozy spaces.

Most of Lovey's kittens grew up at our home in the woods. At one time I counted seventeen cats in the place, even though we were very generous in sharing them with our family and friends, or a rumored friend-of-a-friend's friend.

Before Lovey's next-to-last bunch of kittens arrived, she became bigger and bigger until she looked like she had swallowed a soccer ball. When she finally gave birth, there were eight kittens. Four were calico-colored like Lovey, and the other four were a variety of colors.

When all of them tried to eat at the same time, the bigger ones would crowd out the smaller ones. While Lovey was out on a hunting trip, we fixed a second box and put the four calico kittens in it. When she came back inside the garage/family room, she carefully looked over the new housing arrangements and accepted the two-box system. After that she divided her time between the two boxes. We referred to one box as the "Calico Room" and the other as the "Nursing Home."

The eight kittens must have worn her out. Her last litter was only two babies. When they were about three weeks old, I left for church one afternoon driving our pickup. I stopped at a restaurant thirty-five miles from home, and when I opened the truck door, something fell out onto the parking lot. It was one of the little kittens! When I put it back in the truck, I found the other one behind the seat. Our pickup had been parked out by the trash barrel that afternoon, and Lovey must have moved them in when the doors were left open.

I was thirty-five miles from home, and still twenty miles away from church. I wouldn't be going back home for several hours and faced a whole evening trying to care for two tiny nursing kittens that barely had their eyes open. I went on to church and while I was there, I spooned some diluted milk into their mouths several times. When I returned home, Lovey was sitting in the driveway looking for the mobile home she had moved her family into. She was glad to see me coming down our road and turning into the driveway.

After that episode, we were careful about keeping all vehicle windows rolled up and the doors closed. Even then, while the kittens were still small enough for her to carry around, I always checked behind the seat before I left home.

We never learned what finally became of Lovey. When she failed to show up to eat, we searched for her but couldn't find her. We lived in a thick forest in the country, surrounded by farmland. She enjoyed complete freedom to wander around, as I don't like to keep animals cooped up inside of a building. One summer day she had unexpectedly limped into our lives, and twelve summers later she simply walked out.

Lovey has her special place in our hearts. She was a member of our family, and she can never be replaced.

End of an Era

Ellen Vayo

After I check in, I choose the only secluded seat in the waiting room—the chair between the giant stuffed Saint Bernard and the equally large aquarium, the chair farthest from the commotion of fidgety children, frustrated mothers, and quivering dogs on short leashes.

Across from me, a young woman with a pinched-in waist strokes a kitten. I want to tell her to appreciate the wild-eyed, tiny puff of fur batting at her gaudy Christmas earrings. *That kitten will never again be the same as it is right this moment, never as playful, fur never as shiny, reflexes never as fast.*

Beginnings are such fun. I wish my Molly were a kitten again, with life brightly stretching out in front of her. Funny how I didn't notice the years passing so quickly. Didn't notice Father Time robbing me of the tiny, half-drowned kitten I'd pulled from the river and fed with an eyedropper.

I turn from the kitten with a future and read the titles of the brochures tucked into the plastic holder attached to the wall. Molly shifts beneath the Garfield blanket on my lap, pokes her head out, gazes at me and mews, soundlessly. I rub her ears and start her purr-motor. "You've been a good friend, Molly Gocatly. You're a splendidly worn cat."

I tilt Molly's head upward and kiss her mottled kitty-cat lips. She nuzzles into me, wraps her yellow paws around my hand—and puts a big dent in my heart. "We've always been there for one another, haven't we old girl?"

Molly was my cuddly warmth through the loss of my breasts, a near divorce, and empty nest syndrome. When Molly gave birth to her only litter, I was in the closet with her. I nursed her through spaying, hair-balls, and feline acne.

I catch the woman with the pinched-in waist staring at me. She forces a half smile and averts her gaze. *The young never think they'll grow old, never think their kittens will mellow. I wish that weren't so wrong.*

I gaze down at the cat I've shared a pillow with for more years than I've been married. The cat whose name is included at the end of all my letters and who once received a credit card with a thousand dollar limit.

"Molly." I jiggle the treasure on my lap. "Molly, remember how you loved to ride on the dashboard?" Rode there, in the sunlight, from Point Barrow, Alaska, to the Texas oil fields.

"Remember the winter we were so broke?" We lived on macaroni and cheese for breakfast, lunch, and dinner. Yuck! Thought we'd get the scurvy.

"And remember how I cried when we had to give up that warm, cozy farmhouse and move into that drafty, makeshift trailer?" The move didn't bother Miss Molly Gocatly. Cats know how to adjust. She just climbed into the bottom of my sleeping bag and stayed there until she heard an envelope of cheese being ripped open.

Molly was easy. She never demanded more than a spot of sunlight and a good old belly rub. In turn, she rewarded us with stiffened squirrels at our feet, frightened, peeping birds on our pillows, and, once and once only, a rat in my bubble bath.

My old Molly has slept on the kitchen table for so many years I've come to think of her as a centerpiece. She's always in the midst of everything: lying on the edge of the bathtub dipping her tail into the suds, chasing water beads as they roll down the shower door, sitting on the washer talking cat talk while I fold laundry, walking the countertop while dinner is being prepared, chasing the broom, the dust rag, the vacuum cord. She's the first to greet company when the doorbell rings. *How can life be without my Molly?* I stroke the mass of love on my lap, feel her ribs, her sharp spine.

"Molly Gocatly, wake up," I say louder than I've intended. She opens her eyes and purrs but doesn't lift her head. "Molly, remember the fit you threw when I left on my honeymoon without you? Remember how you broke my only lamp, shredded the drapes, ate two of Roy's goldfish, and terrorized old Peep-Peep into a featherless lump of lunacy?"

The receptionist steps through the door holding a chart and glances around the room. I wince. My breath is caught somewhere between my throat and the pit of my stomach. I feel as though my heart just flipped over backwards. "Miss Roberts," she says. "We're ready for Sweety Pie. Room two." The woman with the pinched-in waist stands and walks by, smiling, with her kitten clutched to her.

Molly's damp nose touches my hand. My breath comes back in jagged gasps. *Ooof,* I hear myself sigh. *I'm not ready for this. I can't do it.* I stand and gather Molly to my chest. Her body twitches. She moans and stares up at me. I run my nose through her fur, breathe in the soft scent of perfumed litter and the stench of pain. *I don't want to do this, but I can't let her go on suffering. She's been too good a friend.* We settle back into the chair next to the aquarium, beneath the stare of the oversized stuffed dog.

"Now what was I saying, Molly? Oh yeah, the honeymoon, old Peep-Peep. Remember how you hid under the bed for days, pouting? Wouldn't come out even for sardines." Good old Molly, when she finally came out, she pooped in Roy's work boots, and then scooted across the paperwork he had strewn on the kitchen table. Molly probably never knew that I saved two of her nine lives that day.

"Sue, we're ready for you." The receptionist studies the papers on her clipboard. She doesn't look at us. She can't. She knows us too well. "Room three," she says. "Doctor will be right with you." I swallow and nod. I stand, but I can barely make my feet move.

I take a seat in room three. My nostrils flare. The room smells of urine, disinfectant, and fear. I arrange Molly on my lap, fuss with the Garfield blanket that covers her, and scratch her throat. Through the wall, I hear a woman laugh. I lean sideways to pick up on the muffled, one-sided conversation being held in baby talk. "You'll never grow old, will you my silly Sweety Pie?"

I kiss Molly between the ears and nod my head toward the wall. "Youth in denial," I say. That woman's joy comes naturally. She's grateful her kitten just needs shots, maybe worming, but is all the same healthy.

Dr. Peters comes in, closes the door behind her, and leans back against it. She stuffs her hands into the pockets of her medical jacket. A white ring circles her mouth. She doesn't like this part of her job. The bantering and niceties we usually exchange are shelved; instead, she asks if I'd like to wait in my car. "I'll bring her to you when I'm finished."

I say nothing. I try, but I can't speak. I shake my head. She turns away, fills a hypodermic syringe with solution, taps it, and pushes the plunger. Fluids spray into the air.

I squeeze my prize. "Good-bye, Molly Gocatly," I say, soundlessly. She mews and gazes up at me. Her eyes are soft and yielding, clouded with cataracts and trust.

Siafu

Roger A. Caras

Every now and then there is one very special animal that crosses over the bridge in a way that is truly magical. That bridge, of course, is the one that spans the chasm that naturally exists between our species and all others. Animal people—animal lovers (why not?)—try to cross that bridge as often as possible. Some few individual animals make it easy, or at least a great deal easier. They come more than halfway. They reach out as we reach out and we succeed in touching each other.

What made Siafu so special? I am not sure. He was the only one of his litter that we kept. That could be part of it. He was clearly the runt, and he was somehow injured when he was a day or two old and developed a large abscess in his right shoulder. He started out being needy and perhaps that had something to do with his special appeal. He needed a nurturing family, and he had one. We were all well matched at the outset.

The infected pocket that went all the way to the joint required flushing with a syringeful of saline solution every few hours and therefore entailed a great deal of handling. When the infection was finally defeated by large doses of antibiotics—Siafu would have a limp and a strange toe-out gait for the rest of his life—Jill and my mother-in-law, Phyllis, were determined to make the tiny kitten into the most highly socialized cat of all time. They did it, in fact, with the entire litter. They took turns. The kittens were held, stroked, carried, touched and touched and touched some more. It worked. They were all incredible cats. Siafu, "Little Biting Ant" in Swahili, was soon the only one left. People continued to remark about the others a decade later. Each was "the most remarkable cat I have ever known." It was simply a matter of intense, deliberate socialization. I am convinced it can be done with any domestic cat, if the holding and petting starts on its first day of life. The natural condition for that cat becomes intense human contact.

Siafu (and this is true of his littermates as well) had something else going in his favor. He was an American Shorthair Silver Ash tabby, and wearing that name requires very specific "beauty" points. On his sides he had perfect bull's-eye targets, concentric diminishing circles of silver and black. (Inexplicably, as he got older, that jet black lightened into a lustrous dark brown and even that was changing toward a kind of reddish gold as a wash on the longest hairs when he died.) On his throat he had three unbroken strands of beads, black on silver. On the front of his forehead there was a perfect M and on the back of his neck an equally perfect butterfly. Crossbandings on his forelegs completed his distinctive markings and added up to a perfectly beautiful cat. He had a round, intense little face, and as his initial runt status predicted he never did grow to be very large. He got rounder as he got older, but he remained a small and very huggable cat, who loved to be hugged. As soon as he was picked up he went limp. Clearly he loved it and was wholly at ease. No question, Siafu with his sweet temper and splendid good looks made everybody love him.

The little tabby made the transition from East Hampton to Thistle Hill Farm with no problem at all. He was so people-oriented that anything was fine with him as long as his people were at hand. After the required indoor imprinting period, he began to explore outside with the rest of the curious crew, and curious they truly were. But he was at the back door asking to come in before sundown every day. He was more than imprinted; it was as if he were attached to the house and his family by a bungee cord.

Eventually the widening rings of exploration he was making around the house included the barn, and he spent a part of each day, as far as we know, with Cosette and Jean Valjean. Since he and Jean Valjean were both males (even though both were neutered) there was a brief ceremonial standoff with some halfhearted spitting. It was strictly pro forma. Siafu was a dream of a cat, a true pussycat, but he was never a wimp. The big-man-on-campus nonsense never amounted to anything. Siafu became, by all odds, the handsomest part-time barn cat anyone ever saw. Unlike the Siamese ladies, he was not a snob.

Siafu loved dogs, and any one of ours that plopped down for a rest was sure to have Siafu arching and rubbing under its chin and marking it with the glands at the corners of his mouth. The purring was intense. He curled up with any dog at hand. And when one of the younger dogs decided to maul him he just rolled over and the more drool the dog deposited on his coat the louder Siafu purred. I worried about him. He was so absolutely trusting he was vulnerable. Clearly he never believed that anyone or anything in this world would hurt him. Happily he was not to be betrayed. Nothing visible ever did.

We never knew Siafu's Thistle Hill beat to go any further than the barn. He would swing by there, visit with Cosette and his pal Jean Valjean (for the two males—they were apparently about the same age—did become friends), and then it was back down toward the house. As far as we know he didn't go back as far as the woods, nor was he ever seen going to or from the streams. I saw him at the edge of the marsh directly behind the house, but I never saw him in it or on any other side of it.

In the house he liked time on the windowsill or one of the banquettes in the kitchen. That is the center of activities, as is any country kitchen. That's where the macaws' very large cages are and where the human traffic is. Somebody is always asking somebody if they would like a cup of coffee or tea, and the kitchen table is where it all happens. Ninety-five percent of our meals are taken in the kitchen rather than in the dining room. And that all suited Siafu perfectly.

Siafu never bit anyone and never scratched anyone intentionally. That is normal for a well-adjusted pet. But he went far beyond not committing negative acts; he wallowed in the positive act of loving. He was wonderful with our grand-children even when they each in turn went through the uncivilized year between roughly two and three. We stopped any mauling as soon as it was detected, but however much of it there was he tolerated, and purred.

To say that Siafu never had his doubts about another animal is not quite true. Friend Vicki Croke, an ace writer-journalist with the Boston Globe, frequently travels with her dog, Lacy. Naturally, she expects a big welcome for her pet here. Everyone does. I'll wager that if a member of either the Anheuser or the Busch family came to stay they'd bring eight or ten Clydesdales with them.

Vicki is not a large lady, not at all. In fact she is rather on the diminutive side. That makes it a little difficult to explain Lacy who, although a dog, is the size, approximately, of a Bactrian camel. Lacy is a true giant, an Irish wolfhound. It can be fun to try to analyze people and their pets. What in this animal appeals to that person? It is very obvious in some cases such as the closet wimp who avails himself of an attack-trained Rottweiler as an extension of an imagined self. But Vicki and the Hound of the Baskervilles! In fact, Lacy is a very sweet dog, sweet and vulnerable, but big—big-time, industrial-strength big.

The first time Vicki brought "the moose" down to Thistle Hill was, I think, something of a shock for poor Siafu. We were in the kitchen about to have coffee and try to decide how Vicki could have possibly misinterpreted my flawless instructions on how to get here from Boston. There was no room for Lacy to stretch out on the kitchen floor and retain the freezer and refrigerator, not to mention the stove, so she was banished to the hall just outside the kitchen door. Siafu had apparently been sleeping upstairs and heard the rise in volume Vicki's arrival elicited. (It is perfectly natural for sound level to go up when people are arriving or departing.)

Lacy was spread out like a shaggy nine-by-twelve-foot rug at the foot of the stairs when Siafu came down to get in on the good stuff going on in the kitchen. On the last step he suddenly became aware of the new dog and stepped down for a little sniffing and perhaps even some snuggling. Lacy was not conditioned to cats and was not sure whether she was supposed to ignore them, salute them, or eat them. She stood up slowly, never taking her eyes off Siafu.

Siafu watched in utter amazement as the largest creature he would probably ever see bearing the dog smell opened like an extension ladder. His eyes seemed to get wider (they probably didn't), and he let loose with one loud yowl, shot between Lacy's legs, and vanished back up the stairs with Lacy staring after him in amazement. For the rest of her stay, Siafu stalked Lacy one floor up, moving from rail post to rail post, peering down and trying to keep the monster in view. I am sure it was nothing more than a game. On her second visit some months later, Siafu apparently forgave Lacy her size and walked through the gray redwood forest of her legs without concern.

As would appear obvious, Siafu was a very contented cat. He could make a game of something unusual like Lacy's obscene size. In fact it almost seemed as if he had a flair for the dramatic. He probably would have been a leading man if he had been human. He was pleased by physical contact as he had been conditioned to be since his first day among us. (He was born in a box in our bedroom. That's among us.) Everything about life pleased him immensely.

He was about ten when feline leukemia struck. He was one of the three the serum somehow did not protect. One life form that Siafu's handsome good looks and wonderful disposition could not charm was a virus, and that is what causes leukemia in cats. Along with Cosette and Fluffy Louise he suddenly stopped eating. In a day his coat looked rough and out of condition. He was listless and ran a fever. His nose and his eyes had discharges and when there was only one thing left to do, we did it.

I guess multiple pet owners really shouldn't have favorites any more than parents should. But that is a theoretical state of purity I have not been able to achieve when considering animals. I have had favorites among our animals, lifetime favorites, and Siafu was at the top of my cat list with perhaps two or three others. I have probably had close to fifty cats in my life, so the top three or four rank high indeed. There never will be a time when I can think of Siafu and not miss him. Together we crossed that bridge and we met somewhere near the middle.